Annulment.
The Wedding That Was

How the Church Can Declare a Marriage Null

Michael Smith Foster

PAULIST PRESS
New York/Mahwah, N.J.

Nihil Obstat: Rev. Msgr. Richard G. Cunningham, JCD
✠ Imprimatur: Bernard Cardinal Law
April 30, 1998

Cover design by Cynthia Dunne

Interior design by Joseph E. Petta

LIBRARY OF CONGRESS CATALOGING-IN-PUBLICATION DATA

Foster, Michael S. (Michael Smith)
    Annulment, the wedding that was : how the church can declare a marriage null / Michael S. Foster.
      p. cm.
    Includes bibliographical references and index.
    ISBN 0–8091–3844–1 (alk. paper)
    1. Marriage—Annulment (Canon law)—Popular works. I. Title.
LAW
262.9′4—dc21   98–44177
                                                               CIP

Published by Paulist Press
997 Macarthur Boulevard
Mahwah, New Jersey 07430

www.paulistpress.com

Printed and bound in the
United States of America

CONTENTS

Part IV: The Church As Witness

Acknowledgments

The author would like to thank his Eminence, Bernard Cardinal Law, Archbishop of Boston, for the opportunity to minister within the Church's judiciary.

The author is grateful for the assistance afforded him in this process by fellow canonists and experts in Church law. I am particularly indebted to Rev. Msgr. Richard G. Lennon, Assistant for Canonical Affairs, Archdiocese of Boston; Sr. Margaret L. Sullivan, C.S.J., J.C.L., Judge of the Boston Metropolitan Tribunal; and Rev. Francis G. Morrisey, o.m.i., J.C.D., Canon Law faculty member of St. Paul University, Ottawa, Ontario.

I am likewise appreciative for the editorial assistance of Mr. Dennis McManus of Paulist Press and Mrs. Barbara Murphy of Newton, Massachusetts.

INTRODUCTION

There Was a Wedding Ceremony, But Did a Marriage Come About That Day?

That is the question brought every day before Church tribunals around the world. In the Latin Church, the ministers of marriage are the bride and the groom. A valid marriage comes into existence at the wedding ceremony when they exchange consent through their wedding vows. This presumption of validity is part of Church law. However, as with any legal presumption, in any legal system it will yield to contrary evidence.

The Wedding That Was...the Case of John and Susan:

Here is what you know: Let's suppose you were a friend of the groom's mother. You had attended the Catholic wedding of John and Susan in 1970. It was a beautiful nuptial mass. Both Susan and John looked so happy. The reception was one of the best parties you had ever attended. The couple had been blessed with a son, John Jr., who was born within the first year of marriage.

1

Unfortunately, the marriage only lasted eight years when John and Susan divorced. Now, ten years later, you have just heard that the Church declared the marriage null. You can't believe it! You saw Susan walk down the aisle that day. You heard both John and Susan, as the ministers of marriage, say, "I do." Susan and John were married and had a child. How can the Church declare the marriage null? It's preposterous! Or, is it?

Here is what you didn't know: The tribunal investigation surrounding the proceedings for a declaration of nullity uncovered the following facts. John and Susan were eighteen-year-old seniors in high school in 1970. They had dated for only four months when she discovered she was pregnant. When she told her parents, they responded: "You have to get married. There is no question about it!" Her parents insisted that for the sake of the child she had to marry her boyfriend.

Susan had thought about her parents' directive for a few days. She then went back to them and said: "I don't want to get married. I'm only eighteen. John is only eighteen. I don't love him and I'm certain he doesn't love me. I'll have the baby without question, but there is no way I will go through with a wedding!"

Her parents responded in anger by saying, "Fine! It's your decision. You're an adult and we can't make you get married. However, if you don't get married, we don't ever want to see you again. Good-bye, good luck, you are on your own. That's how strongly we feel as adults regarding the legitimacy of our first grandchild!"

So the circumstances were: Susan was eighteen, pregnant and going to be thrown out of the house and abandoned with an infant **unless** she went through with a wedding ceremony. It was under those circumstances that she walked down the aisle that day. As she told the court, "I smiled all day and no one knew what I was really feeling."

Most everyone at the church thought this was a wonderful experience for Susan. As soon as Susan had stood up publicly and said, "I do," those in attendance and the community of the faithful at large presumed a valid sacrament of marriage had come into existence. The Church presumed that Susan, as the minister, meant what she said; otherwise, why would she have said it?

In the proceedings before the tribunal Susan was able to prove that she only married under the directives of her parents due to her fear of being abandoned with a child. Her brother knew of the exchange between her parents, as did her two best friends. Through the corroboration of witness testimonies the fear brought to bear on Susan's consent was substantiated. So, after the testimonies of the witnesses had been collected and the legal arguments of various court officials had been put forward, the marriage was declared null by the Church on the ground of force and fear.

Everyone in the church on that wedding day had seen this young bride walk down the aisle. Everyone had heard Susan, as one of the ministers, say, "I do." However, after the tribunal had examined the facts and circumstances surrounding this minister's consent, it was clear that she was pressured to act against her will.

The *Catechism of the Catholic Church* states: "The consent must be an act of the will of each of the contracting parties, free of coercion or grave external fear. No human power can substitute for this consent. If this freedom is lacking, the marriage is invalid."[1] Church teaching is clear; the sacrament of marriage can only be brought about by a free act of the will. Therefore, there was no exchange of valid consent and thus the sacrament had not come into existence at John and Susan's wedding, as the community of the faithful had presumed.

In coming to a judgment regarding the nullity of a marriage, tribunal officials examine all of the facts. They assess these facts in view of the Church's teachings and laws on marriage. There are many checks and balances in the Church's procedural laws. The decision of one judge is always analyzed by other judges. The judgments of one court are always reviewed by an appellate court. The community of the faithful is asked to respect these judgments, remembering the courts alone have all the facts.

A Process Understood by Few

The Church's process for declaring a marriage null is mysterious to most people. Church laws regarding confidentiality prevent open discussion about any case. While a declaration of nullity is a matter of record in the Church, the facts of the case are confidential. The records, which include the ground(s) on which the annulment was granted, are sealed. This confidentiality is meant to protect the good name and reputation of all the parties involved. Yet, such confidentiality inevitably leads to speculation and misconceptions. The Church is cognizant of the tremendous confusion over annulments, but its required silence on individual cases should not be interpreted as an insensitive dismissal of sincere questioning.

This book is intended to demystify the concepts and the procedures surrounding annulments. The Church's tribunal proceedings are mysterious to many because they are shrouded in laws written in Latin and concerned with complex matters of theology and procedural law. However, as the answers to the questions contained in this book indicate, neither the theological realities nor the laws are beyond understanding.

This is not a "how-to" book. It will not explain how one should go about petitioning the Church for a declaration of nullity. Nor will it explain "how to" oppose such a petition. Though these types of books exist, they have limited applications because tribunals fulfill Church laws through policies that vary from one tribunal to another due to local circumstances. By design, this book is intended to familiarize a person with the Church's concepts of marriage and its tribunal processes.

Annulments, more aptly called declarations of nullity, have existed in the Church for centuries. Nevertheless, the concept and procedures surrounding declarations of nullity are mysterious to most people. When many people hear about annulment proceedings, images of tribunal inquisitions are conjured up in their minds. Many simply shy away because of a fear of the unknown. For those courageous enough to enter into the Church's court structure, legalities usually associated with civil courts immediately confront them. There are court officials such as judges, defenders and advocates. The parties are afforded procedural rights; there are peremptory time frames; and they have the right to appeal decisions.

This reality of the Church's judicial life is a far cry from the lived experience of most Catholics. Persons dealing with the Church's court system are often struck by the cool and detached manner with which they are treated. They receive formal letters containing legal decrees and often only deal over the phone with individuals they never meet but to whom they reveal very personal information. This is very different from the pastoral reception one finds on the parish level. This is due to the fact that the tribunal process is an impartial search for truth on the part of Church officials. The tribunal declares that the nullity of the marriage has been proven or that it has not been proven. This is a weighty search, as it questions the validity of marriage, that is, that sacred lifelong union which has been instituted by God.

Marriage Is a Public and Private Reality in Both the Church and the State

Some people believe that marriage is purely a private matter. They ask why the Church involves itself. The answer is that the Church, like the State, considers marriage to be a public act, not simply a private matter between two individuals. When two people contract a marriage, a public reality comes into existence. After all, a marriage has many public ramifications for both the Church and civil societies, including the well-being of the spouses, the welfare of children and the cohesive nature of the community as a whole.

If a marriage breaks down, civil divorce often follows. The rise of divorce rates in the United States is clearly troublesome. This is especially so when a divorce involves Catholics, since the Church holds the sacrament of marriage to be indissoluble—a permanent, covenant relationship between God and the spouses.

Once the State dissolves a marriage through divorce, the ex-spouses are free to marry again according to civil law. This is where the two societies diverge. Observing the words of Jesus, the Church holds that no human power can dissolve a valid, consummated sacramental marriage. This truth is enshrined in the Church's theological and canonical traditions.

Some people have challenged the Church's authority to intrude in their lives after a divorce and to make a judgment about the sacramental and/or valid nature of their marriages. Many others have simply misunderstood what an annulment is or how the Church decides to grant one. The debate is about the tribunal process and the Church's domain over all marriages, particularly its teaching on indissolubility.

A Declaration of Nullity Does Not "Dissolve" a Union or "Erase" Reality

Much of the present confusion over annulments is also due to the Church's teaching on indissolubility and its annulment procedures, which are seemingly contradictory. However, these two realities are not in opposition, but rather balance one another. For when the Church teaches what marriage is, it is also teaching what marriage is not.

A declaration of nullity is not a dissolution of marriage; it is not a Church divorce. Rather, it is a judicial finding that a marriage had not been brought about on the wedding day, as the faith community had presumed. The Church's law on marriage is like a coin. On one side there is an exposition of "what marriage is." When the coin is flipped over, the opposite is established—"what marriage is not." This book will address both sides of that coin.

The law declares that marriage is brought about through: (1) the consent of the bride and groom, (2) legitimately manifested, (3) by those qualified according to the law (again, the bride and the groom). So, if the consent was defective—marriage was NOT brought about. If the consent was NOT legitimately manifested—marriage was NOT brought about. If one or both of the persons were unqualified according to law—the marriage was NOT brought about.

When a marriage is declared null, a couple is freed of the presumed "bond" of matrimony because a valid marriage bond had not come into existence on the wedding day. The declaration does not deny that love existed in the relationship or family; more often than not, it did. The wedding ceremony is not wiped away; it clearly occurred. The relationship between the husband and wife and the years they spent together are not wiped away. It is part of their individual and collective history. The children of the union remain legitimate in Church law. A declaration of nullity does not dissolve or erase a marriage, but rather declares a marriage did not come about on the wedding day.

Understanding the Church's Laws on Marriage and Nullity

The Church's rich teachings on marriage find legal expression in the laws of the Church. A Church law is usually referred to as a *canon*. The specific canons or laws on marriage number one hundred and eleven. Admittedly, these laws are both dry and dense. Nonetheless, they are rooted in the theological understanding of marriage.[2]

Some of the Church's laws have been in existence for almost two millennia, and others are derived more recently from the teaching of the Second Vatican Council. These laws and their foundational teachings touch on all marriages to varying degrees, that is, marriages between Roman Catholics, Protestants and non-Christians. In some tribunals of the United States, close to twenty percent of the cases deal with non-Catholics! This book will deal with the legal implications for each type of these marriages.

The Church affords any divorced person the right to petition for a declaration of nullity. Thousands of men and women do so each year, with a slightly higher percent of petitioners being women. The length of the marriage or presence of children does not prevent the acceptance of a petition. Nor does the name or position of the petitioner, respondent or any witness matter. Everyone is accorded the same procedural rights. No one is penalized for being well known, nor for being unknown. Everyone is treated justly and in accord with the norms of law.

This book is intended for anyone interested in learning more about the concept of a Church "annulment": whether single, married, ordained or layperson, students of theology, seminarians, parish ministers, Roman Catholic, Protestant, unbaptized, agnostic or atheist, wife, husband, child or ex-spouse. Hopefully, it will enlighten anyone who has participated in a tribunal investigation, including petitioners, respondents, witnesses, professionals in the mental health fields and civil attorneys. Collectively, the 101 individual questions within this book answer the larger question: Annulment—what is it all about?

PART I:

The Right to Marry

The faith community's understanding of marriage is steeped in two thousand years of theological knowledge. The theology of marriage has developed over the centuries through a broadening of horizons and a bridging of expanses. The writings on marriage could fill libraries. So let the reader beware! Though the following section may be somewhat informative regarding the nullity of marriage, it pales into insignificance in regard to the Church's theology of marriage.

Q. 1. What is marriage?

Marriage is a social institution in which a man and a woman live their lives as husband and wife. It has both private and public ramifications. For Christians, marriage is more than a sociological reality; it is an authentically religious reality. Christians believe that God is the author of marriage and that he has determined its elements and characteristics. In addition, the Church places upon marriage certain conditions that bring it into existence.

As the *Catechism of the Catholic Church* states: "The intimate community of life and love which constitutes the married state has been established by the Creator and endowed by him with its own proper laws....God himself is the author of marriage."[3] As God is the author of all true marriages, so the Church is concerned with the state of marriage in the world—whether sacramental and nonsacramental.

A sacramental marriage is the union of two Christians. In virtue of their baptisms they invite God to enter into their covenant of love. The presence of God's grace in their union effects the reality of Christ's presence in the world. A sacramental marriage is aptly referred to as a **Christian marriage.** A baptized bride and a baptized groom administer this sacrament one to the other; they are the ministers of Christian marriage. The Church's teachings and laws define the nature and purpose of Christian marriage: "The matrimonial covenant, by which a man and a woman establish between themselves a partnership of the whole of life, is by its very nature ordered toward the good of the spouses and the procreation and education of children; this covenant between baptized persons has been raised by Christ the Lord to the dignity of a sacrament."[4]

A nonsacramental marriage occurs either between two unbaptized persons or between a baptized person and an unbaptized person. Since marriage has been created by God, it is both good and a part of the natural order. Hence, a nonsacramental marriage is aptly referred to as a **good and natural marriage.** It is the union of husband and wife, and God enters into this union through grace. His abiding love is present to the spouses, and the marriage is a sign of God's creative love in the world. However, unlike a Christian marriage, a good and natural marriage is not sacramental, that is, an effective sign of Christ's presence in the world; only two baptized ministers can effect this unique presence of Christ. Yet, the nature and purpose of a good and natural marriage are identical to those of a Christian marriage: "The matrimonial covenant, by which a man and a woman establish between themselves a partnership of the whole of life, is by its very nature ordered toward the good of the spouses and the procreation and education of children...."[5]

The Church teaches that both Christian marriages and good and natural marriages are one and indissoluble by the natural law.[6] These two essential properties of unity and indissolubility are rooted in Scripture (cf. Gn 2:24; Mt 19:3–9; Mk 10:2–12; Lk 16:18; 1 Cor 7:2–6, 10–11, 39–40; Eph 5:32; Rom 7:3). These essential properties flow from the very nature of marriage as intended by God. Without these properties there can never be a real marriage. In light of these beliefs the Church readily rejects some cultural forms of "marriage."

Since unity involves the marriage of one man and one woman, marriage is monogamous. This Christian belief in monogamy has often been at odds with other cultures. For instance, any form of polygamy is excluded from being considered as marriage, as it is devoid of the essential element of unity. Polygamy has various forms: one man with several wives (polygyny), one woman with several husbands (polyandry) or several men marrying several women (group marriages). Each of these instances would stand in direct contradiction to the will of God that marriage is monogamous. Thus these unions are not properly marriages in the Church's view.

The Church is not the only society to define marriage and thus reject contrary practices. For instance, the United States government has recently faced a challenge in regard to "same-sex marriages." The fact that the Hawaiian courts have legalized these unions has created concern in the other forty-nine states. Some states have responded with legislation to thwart same-sex marriages. On the federal level the Defense of Marriage Act would define marriage as a legal union between one man and one woman. It would thereby bar the federal government from recognizing same-sex marriages. The bill also protects states from being compelled to honor another state's law or judicial proceeding that recognizes marriages between persons of the same sex.

As the American culture faces the issue of "same-sex marriages" through government, the issue is nondebatable in the Church. Though called marriages by some people, same-sex unions can never be marriages in any real sense because the essential property of unity between one man and one woman is absent. The concept of "same-sex marriages" is an oxymoron.

Clearly, distinct cultures, societies and groups of individuals ascribe different characteristics to the word *marriage*–for example, *a polygamous marriage, an open marriage, a same-sex marriage, a group marriage, a trial marriage.* However, these are not marriages in any real Christian sense. They are merely unions of two or more individuals. The Church admits to two types of marriage: *a Christian marriage* or *a good and natural marriage.*

Q. 2. Who has the right to marry?

Since marriage is a natural state of life, it is open in principle to every man and woman. Even though it is a right based in the natural law, it is not a limitless right. Church law regulates that any person who is not prohibited by law has the right to marry.[7] Consequently, the right to marry may be restricted. Most of these restrictions are referred to as *diriment impediments;* they exist to protect both the individuals involved and the wider community.

A person is incapable of contracting marriage validly under certain circumstances.[8] These are called diriment impediments and there are twelve of them in Church law.[9] Many, though not all, of these impediments can be dispensed prior to the marriage. A dispensation is the relaxation of Church law in a particular case. The proper Church authority will permit a dispensation from the impediment provided the circumstances are appropriate.[10] If the requirement is dispensed, the person is then rendered capable of marriage. *However, if the impediment is not dispensed at the time of the wedding, the marriage is invalid.* In this case everyone at the church may have thought a marriage had come into existence, but it had not. The parties were not qualified for marriage due to the impediment. There was a wedding ceremony, but a marriage did not come about that day.

Q. 3. What prevents a person from marrying in the Church?

The law states that marriage is brought about through: (1) the consent of the bride and groom, (2) legitimately manifested, (3) by those qualified according to the law (again, the bride and the groom).[11] If one or both of the persons was not qualified according to law to place consent, then marriage was NOT brought about.

A great deal of pastoral care and preparation is required before a couple celebrates their marriage.[12] Part of this preparation is concerned with the parties' legal qualifications to enter into marriage. As stated above, some situations prevent a person from marrying validly.

There are two types of impediments: those of divine or natural law and those of Church law.[13] Divine law impediments bind all persons regardless of religious affiliation or lack thereof. Impediments of Church law bind only baptized Roman Catholics or those baptized Christians who have become members of the Catholic Church.

There are three impediments of divine or natural law that prevent any person from marrying validly: certain degrees of consanguinity (family relationships), impotence and prior valid marriages. The first two are precepts of the natural law, while the third is a commandment of the Gospel. The impediments of divine law may not be dispensed. *Any person who marries under these impediments always marries invalidly.*

There are nine impediments designated by Church law that prevent Roman Catholics from marrying validly. Some are personal: age, sacred orders (deacon, priest or bishop), and profession of a public perpetual vow of chastity in a religious institute (religious sisters, brothers and priests). Others are situational: marriage to an unbaptized person (disparity of cult); abduction; the crime of murder (for the sake of marriage or murder conspiracy); certain degrees of blood relationships, that is, in-law relationships (affinity); relationships established by concubinage; and relationships from adoption. These impediments prohibit a person from marrying validly. They may however be dispensed by the proper Church authority. In fact all Church law impediments may be dispensed provided the circumstances are appropriate. If a dispensation is granted, the persons may validly marry.

Q. 4. Is a divorced person free to marry in the Church regardless of a prior marriage?

No.

The impediment of a valid, prior bond of marriage renders a person incapable of marriage.[14] This impediment is based in both natural and divine law. It is rooted in the essential properties of marriage, unity and indissolubility. The impediment exists if two conditions are met. First, the prior marriage was valid, that is, it has not been declared invalid by Church authority. Second, the prior bond still exists according to Church law, that is, it has not been dissolved by the death of one of the spouses or by Church authority.[15] If these conditions are in place, the impediment of prior bond of marriage cannot be dispensed.

Unfortunately, it happens that some individuals lie about previous marriages when they wish to marry again. If, in fact, a person marries while bound to a previous marriage, the wedding is legally meaningless. Though premarital investigations attempt to address this type of deception, they are not always successful. As an aside, you may read in the parish bulletin that two individuals are soon to be married. These are called the banns of marriage. This is more than a social announcement. It is a legal observance designed to ascertain the freedom of both parties to marry. Remember, many laws exist simply in response to abuses. Sadly, people are not always honest about past marriages.

Q. 5. What is meant by the impediment of impotence?

One of the ends of marriage is the procreation of children. Hence, potency on the part of the man and woman is necessary. For the man this includes (1) the erection of the penis, (2) its penetration into the vagina and (3) ejaculation. For the woman it includes (1) the possession of the vagina and (2) the capacity to receive the penis into it. If any of these essential requirements of potency is absent, then the impediment of impotence exists.[16] The impediment is based in the laws of nature, as impotency is the incapacity to perform sexual intercourse in a natural way. It affects all persons regardless of religious affiliation or lack thereof.

In order to invalidate marriage, the law requires that the impotence existed at the time of the marriage ceremony, that is, it did not come about after the wedding. In addition, it must be "legally perpetual"—meaning that it cannot be cured or overcome. A person may be impotent with any person of the opposite sex, that is, *absolute* impotence. Or, a person may be impotent simply with the chosen spouse, that is, *relative* impotence; for example, there may be a gross disproportion in size between the sexual organs of the parties.

If the existence of impotence is in any way doubtful, then the impediment is considered nonexistent at the time of consent. The law on impotence also states that sterility is not the same as impotence, and is not an impediment to marriage.

Suppose John and Susan are both Episcopalian. They marry and then divorce. Susan now wishes to marry a Roman Catholic, but is unable to do so because of her prior marriage to John. She alleges John's impotence at the time of consent. A tribunal investigation, primarily through medical records, proves that this was indeed the case. Since John was impotent, he was not legally qualified to marry. The marriage would be declared null by virtue of the diriment impediment of impotence. Susan would no longer be bound to the union and would be free to marry in the Catholic Church.

Q. 6. If a man and woman are related to one another, can they marry?

Preexisting relationships between the parties may also render individuals incapable of marriage. The impediment of consanguinity is based on blood relationship.[17] Most societies and legal systems have a prohibition on marriage between close blood relatives. The reasons are possible genetic consequences, as well as the desire to protect the sanctity of the family in its already established relationships. The blood relationships that impede marriage are well defined in law. There are impediments based on the direct line in blood relationship (father/daughter), and others based on the collateral line relationship (brother/sister).

Some relational impediments are considered to be of divine law. They affect the baptized and unbaptized, and are never dispensed. These would be permanent blood relationships, that is, father/daughter, grandmother/grandson. So, for example, King Oedipus could never have validly married his mother! Lesser blood relationships are of Church law and may be dispensed for serious reasons. So marriage may be permitted, after dispensation, between an uncle/niece, aunt/nephew or first cousins.

An impediment to marriage also arises from the relationships established through marriage, that is, in-law relationships.[18] Called the impediment of affinity, it invalidates marriage with the blood relations of a partner. It exists only in the direct line of relationship; so a stepfather may not marry his stepdaughter. Since this is an impediment of Church law, it binds only Catholics and it may be dispensed for serious reasons. The impediment does not exist in the collateral line. So a man may marry the sister of his deceased wife.

The impediment of public propriety is similar to that of affinity. Yet where affinity (an in-law relationship) arises from a valid marriage, the impediment of public propriety arises between two people who live together as husband and wife without the benefit of a legal or formal marriage. They are either in an invalid marriage or simply living together. The impediment of public propriety is established by Church law; it invalidates marriage with the blood relations of a partner only in the direct line.[19] So a woman living with a man cannot validly marry his father or his son.

Finally, there is an impediment that arises through adoption.[20] Children who have been adopted in civil law are considered to be the children of the adoptive parents in canon law.[21] The impediment of adoption effects the same relationships as the impediment of consanguinity; so a man cannot marry his adopted daughter. However, the two impediments do differ. If the civil court order that established the adoptive relationship ceased, then the impediment would also cease to exist. Obviously, the biological relationship of consanguinity can never be terminated. Also, as adoption is an impediment of Church law, theoretically, it can be dispensed. However, the circumstances here would indeed be rare.

Q. 7. How old do you have to be to marry validly?

In order for any person to marry validly, the natural law stipulates their having attained puberty. So the Church would not recognize the marriage of two eight-year-olds as valid, regardless of the cultural acceptance of such child marriages. In addition, Church law stipulates a specific age requirement for Catholics to marry validly. You may be amazed to hear that it is fourteen for a girl and sixteen for a boy![22] The law of the Church is worldwide. As hard as it is to believe, these ages are acceptable in some cultures. So the law is clear—if a Catholic below the stated age in universal law attempts marriage, he or she does so invalidly. Now let's suppose a young man claims to be eighteen years old when in fact he is five days short of his sixteenth birthday. He marries an eighteen-year-old woman. The Catholic wedding is lovely and everyone rightly presumes a marriage has come into existence.

A year later the couple divorces. The woman wishes to remarry, but is unable to do so because her prior bond is presumed to be valid. If she is able to prove in a Church court that the groom was not of legal age at the time of consent, the marriage would be declared null due to the impediment of age. A review of both the marriage record and his birth record would establish the existence of the impediment. Hence, the legal presumption that this was a valid marriage would yield to a declaration of nullity. The groom was in fact incapable by law of placing (giving) consent, as he was not of legal age.

It should be noted that the universal law allows the bishops of a nation or a region to establish a higher age as a requirement for marriage. However, if this higher age is not observed, the marriage would only be illegal, not invalid.

Q. 8. Can a Roman Catholic marry a person of another faith who is not baptized?

Yes.

However, a Catholic who wishes to marry an unbaptized person must first receive a dispensation from the impediment of disparity of cult. The dispensation is required if the marriage is to be recognized as valid in the Church.[23] Keep in mind that for a Christian marriage, both ministers (the bride and groom) are to be baptized Christians. When one of the parties is unbaptized, a dispensation from disparity of cult is required, and the resulting marriage is nonsacramental. It is a good and natural marriage, but since it is nonsacramental it lacks the "particular firmness" of a Christian marriage.[24]

Every law has an underlying value. At stake here is the continued faith of the Catholic party and the initiation of future children into the Catholic Church. In view of these values, when requesting the dispensation from this impediment, the Catholic party is made aware of his or her obligations to the Catholic faith as well as the consequent responsibility to baptize and educate the children into the faith. As the *Catechism of the Catholic Church* states, this dispensation: "...presupposes that both parties know and do not exclude the essential ends and properties of marriage and the obligations assumed by the Catholic party concerning the baptism and education of the children in the Catholic Church."[25]

If Cathy, a Catholic, marries John, a Buddhist, and she had not obtained the dispensation from disparity of cult, the Church does not recognize the marriage as valid. She was impeded from marrying him validly because of the impediment of disparity of cult. By deciding not to request the dispensation, she neglected her responsibilities to the faith community and opted to marry outside the Church.

Q. 9. What happens if a priest, religious sister or brother marries; is it valid?

The impediment of sacred orders invalidates the marriage of any deacon, priest or bishop who has not been dispensed from the obligations of celibacy.[26] This is an impediment of Church law with religious significance. When a man is ordained in the Latin Church, he freely embraces the law of celibacy (some permanent deacons are exceptions).[27] In other words, he may not marry. Once he has vowed to live the life of a celibate, he cannot simply walk away from this promise and marry at will. A man is bound to his promise of celibacy, just as a man or woman is bound to the perpetual vow of chastity in religious life.[28]

In order to marry validly, an ordained man would first have to obtain a decree of laicization, which frees him from the obligations associated with the ordained ministry. This decree usually includes the dispensation from the law of celibacy. The power to dispense from this impediment is reserved to the pope.[29]

So, in the well-known book, *The Thorn Birds,* had Father Ralph married Meg secretly in a Church service, deceiving the officiating priest about his true identity, no marriage would have come into existence. He was not qualified by law to give consent for marriage because of the impediment of sacred orders.

Another impediment established by Church law with religious significance is a public, perpetual vow of chastity in a religious institute.[30] All of the adjectival restrictions must be present. Since diriment impediments restrict the natural law right to marry, they are to be interpreted strictly. Not all vows of chastity render one incapable of marriage. The vow has to be made publicly,[31] not privately. It is a perpetual vow, not a temporary vow. It is made in a religious institute, not in other institutes of consecrated life.[32] The power to dispense from this impediment is reserved to the pope if the person belongs to a religious community of pontifical right.[33] If the institute is that of diocesan right, the bishop can dispense from the impediment.[34]

So let us suppose that Sister Martha of Boston travels around the country a great deal in her apostolate. She meets and, over time, falls in love with a man from Denver. She neglects to tell him she is a religious sister! She also fails to mention this to the priest who is going to officiate at their wedding in Denver. The priest, like the groom, is completely taken by Sister Martha's charismatic personality. He doesn't follow through on the necessary paperwork to determine her freedom to marry, and the wedding occurs. Everyone at the church assumes they have just witnessed a marriage.

A month later Sister Martha can no longer live with her deception and confesses the truth. The marriage is declared null because she was rendered incapable by law of placing consent due to the impediment of a public, perpetual vow of chastity in a religious institute.[35]

Q. 10. What crimes before marriage prevent a person from marrying in the Church?

There are two Church laws that render a person incapable of marriage due to unlawful acts. The first is the impediment of abduction.[36] The law states that no marriage can exist if a woman has been abducted or detained against her will for the purpose of marriage. The drafters of the law were conscious of the fact that abduction was not as infrequent throughout the world as one might think.

Abduction and detention involve two different types of violence against women. In one instance the violence may be physical: for example, she may be locked in a room until she "gives in" to a marriage. It could also be moral violence, that is, she may be pressured by threats to consent to marriage. In either instance the impediment comes into existence and the resulting marriage is invalid. The law states that the impediment ceases to exist when the woman has separated from her abductor and is in a safe, secure and free place. Since the law stipulates the cessation of the impediment, it would be illogical to request or grant a dispensation from it.

The second act that Church law defines as rendering a person incapable of marriage due to an unlawful act is murder. It is, more technically, the act of coniugicide, the murder of one's husband or wife or the husband or wife of the intended spouse. This act brings about the impediment of "crime."[37] The parameters of this impediment are strictly defined in Church law.

Since murder is the cause of the impediment, the act must be completed and not merely attempted. There are two scenarios related to the impediment of crime. In the first scenario, the murder is committed against the person's present spouse for the purpose of marrying another; or, it is committed against the other's spouse, again, for the purpose of marriage.[38] So murder for the reasons of self-defense or even financial gain would not bring about the impediment. Whether the murder is committed personally or through the agency of others, the guilty party is rendered incapable of marriage. The impediment bars the marriage between the murderer and the intended—so the murderer is legally free to marry anyone else!

If Otto murders Ivan in order to marry Audrey, the moment Ivan dies, the impediment between Otto and Audrey arises. This is true even if Audrey knows nothing about Otto's desire to marry, or his crime. Should they marry, they do so invalidly due to the impediment of crime.

A second scenario regarding the impediment of crime has to do with the mutual cooperation between a man and a woman in bringing about the death of either of their spouses.[39] If such a death occurs, the impediment of crime arises. In this particular case there does not have to be a specific intention or motivation for marriage. So the impediment arises even if the death was not inflicted for the purpose of marriage.

Melanie and Victor own a failing business together. Melanie is married to Midas. Together Melanie and Victor conspire and then kill Midas for financial gain. The moment Midas dies the impediment of crime arises between Melanie and Victor, even if they never considered marriage.

Two simple rules of thumb apply to this impediment. In the first case, a murderer who kills for the sake of marriage should not be rewarded with marriage. In the second, criminals cannot marry each other—murder partners cannot be marriage partners! Any dispensation from this impediment is reserved to the pope.[40] Normally, if the murder is publicly known, the dispensation is not given. An exception to this practice can be made if the person petitioning for the dispensation is in danger of death.

Q. 11. What is civil annulment; civil divorce?

A civil annulment is concerned with problems arising prior to the marriage ceremony. It essentially states that the marriage never happened, that is, the marital status never existed. Though the grounds for annulments differ from state to state, there are several common-law grounds that still apply in most states. Certain blood relationships render a marriage null: for example, brother-sister, parent-child, uncle-niece and aunt-nephew marriages. Mental incapacity at the time of the wedding could also be grounds for a civil annulment. In certain instances fraud would be grounds for a civil annulment—for example, lying about one's religion, past criminal record or disease, or hiding a pregnancy. The inability to bear children or to have sexual intercourse may also render a marriage null. Duress at the time of consent also voids a marriage, since one's consent must be voluntary. Being under the prescribed age may also render a party incapable of a civil marriage. The procedure for a civil annulment is similar to that of divorce. The court determines the distribution of assets and liabilities, as well as custody, visitation, child support and alimony.

There are clear similarities between Church declarations of nullity and civil annulments. Both are concerned with issues prior to the marriage, such as the consent of the parties (fraud, mental incapacity and duress) and the legal qualifications of the parties (consanguinity, age and impotence). Furthermore, as with Church declarations of nullity, children born of a civilly annulled marriage are considered legitimate by the State.

A civil divorce differs conceptually from a civil annulment, for it is concerned with problems arising after the marriage ceremony. In effect, it terminates the legal marital status. It dissolves the marriage contract. All fifty states allow divorce and each has its own particular requirements.

There are basically two types of divorce—"no fault" and "fault." A "no fault" divorce describes a situation in which one spouse suing for divorce does not have to prove that the other spouse did something wrong. Now with that said, there nonetheless needs to be a reason recognized by the State for the dissolution of a marriage contract. Reasons such as "irreconcilable differences," "incompatibility" and "irremediable breakdown of the marriage" are often acceptable to the State to confirm that the couple can no longer continue in marriage. Therefore the marriage is dissolved. However, in a dozen states it is also required that couples must live apart for months or even years before obtaining a "no fault" divorce.

A "fault" divorce does not require the same period of separation as a "no fault" divorce. So, many people will opt for this form of divorce. In addition, if a spouse can prove that the other is at fault for the breakdown of the marriage, he/she may receive a greater share of the marital property, more alimony or a greater amount of child custody and support. Traditional grounds utilized by courts for "fault" divorces are: cruelty (the inflicting of unnecessary emotional or physical pain), desertion, adultery or prison confinement for a specified number of years. Unlike "no fault" divorces, a spouse can prevent a "fault" divorce by convincing the court that he or she is not at fault. The reasons for preventing "fault" divorces are well defined in civil law.

Q. 12. If the State permits divorce, why won't the Church?

In the words of our Lord from the scriptures it is clear that God willed marriage to be indissoluble (Mt 5:31–32; 19:3–9; Mk 10:9; Lk 16:18; 1 Cor 7:10–11). Indissolubility is a property of both Christian and good and natural marriages.

Divorce implies that the State can dissolve what is in essence indissoluble. But the Church does not recognize the civil dissolution of a marriage. A civil divorce has no legal consequences in Church law. The Church considers both parties bound to the union, though they obviously no longer live together.

The faith community usually considers divorce an offense against the dignity of marriage, whether a Christian or a good and natural marriage, for it brings disorder into the family and society.[41] It is especially injurious to a Christian marriage. It violates the indissolubility inherent in a Christian marriage that mirrors the unbreakable bond between Christ and the Church.[42]

The *Catechism of the Catholic Church* states:

> The Lord Jesus insisted on the original intention of the Creator who willed that marriage be indissoluble. He abrogates the accommodations that had slipped into the old Law. Between the baptized, "a ratified and consummated marriage cannot be dissolved by any human power or for any reason other than death." The Church does not have the power to contravene this disposition of divine wisdom.[43]

The catechism and the law[44] are clear: a consummated and sacramental marriage cannot be dissolved by any power on earth. Simply put, the Church can never permit the dissolution of a valid, sacramental, consummated marriage.

Q. 13. How does the high rate of divorce in the United States affect the Church?

Divorce in the United States is epidemic. Yet, our country is not alone; divorce also increased drastically throughout Australia, Canada and Europe, from the mid-1960s until the mid-1980s. The trend in the United States has not abated. Demographers have analyzed the rates of divorce by grouping together those who have married in a given year, and the figures are staggering. Half of the marriages entered into in the mid-1970s will end in divorce, while 64 percent of marriages entered into more recently will end in divorce![45] Furthermore, there is no empirical evidence to suggest that Catholics divorce at a substantially lower rate than non-Catholics. Presently, divorce is widespread in our society, and its consequences for the faith community are far-reaching.

Almost half of all children in the United States will spend some time in a single-parent family, due primarily to divorce. It is all too frequent that ex-spouses become ex-parents. The time that children spend in a single-parent (usually the mother) home after divorce is, on the average, six years. Divorce can adversely affect children on many levels: economic, behavioral, academic and psychological.

One of children's greatest losses is intangible: that of the child-father bond. The tangible consequences of this primary loss are substantial; a recent survey indicates:

- over one half faced a housing crisis
- 32 percent of the children went hungry
- 55 percent lost access to health care checkups
- 36 percent did not get health care when ill due to cost
- 37 percent lacked appropriate clothing—for example, winter coats
- 57 percent lost regular child care because of the cost
- 49 percent of the children could not afford school activities
- 26 percent were left unsupervised when their mothers went to work
- often, children lost both parents, one who abandoned them, and the other who was gone most of the time working several jobs to attempt to support the family.[46]

Seventy-five percent of divorced mothers and 85 percent of divorced fathers remarry.[47] However, evidence suggests that remarriage neither reproduces nor restores the lost unity of the family. When a mother remarries, the child must adapt to the presence of a stepfather. Children, preadolescents and adolescents all react differently to this new dynamic, and often not well. In fact, half of these remarriages are likely to end in divorce before the children turn eighteen.[48] It is estimated that 15 percent of all children will see their biological/custodial parents divorce, remarry and redivorce before they reach eighteen!

Marriage is the bedrock of the any healthy society, including the society of the Church. The Church calls the family the "domestic church." The family is where spouses live out their vocation of marital love and support, and where children are nurtured and loved and taught the faith. Clearly, the epidemic of divorce and its effects on our children and adults are of paramount concern for the Church.

Q. 14. How can the Church respond to the needs of the divorced?

One obvious response of the Church to the high rates of divorce is to develop preventative measures against divorce. Much of the Church's concern for healthy marriage preparation arises out of its concern for the escalation of divorce rates around the world. The Church has been a societal leader in its premarital instruction and preparation of couples for marriage. Marriage preparation is required for engaged couples, and it exists on parish, diocesan and regional levels around the country. Proper preparation for their sacred commitment is critical. The Church has a tremendous concern for brides and grooms since they are the ministers of marriage who will embrace and live out the sacrament in the world.

The obligations of the community of the faithful to assist

the couple do not cease on the wedding day. The family is the domestic church; as such, spouses need support as they grow in mutual love. When they are gifted by God with children, they need assistance in parenting skills. Most dioceses offer programs of support for couples and families, such as marriage enhancement, natural family planning education, children's catechetical instruction, adult education and much more.

Families need support from the Church in times of difficulties as well. Marriage is a lived human reality. It is not an ideal beyond attainment. Since it is a human endeavor, it is affected by the reality of sin. In fact, the first sin had as its consequence the rupture of the original communion between the first man and woman. Marriage may be threatened by "...discord, a spirit of domination, infidelity, jealousy and conflicts that can escalate into hatred and separation."[49] The consequences of these sins and others like them are evidenced today in marital difficulties, separation, divorce and civil remarriage. It is the responsibility of the Church to aid and support its members in troubled marriages.

Spouses who have separated and divorced suffer a tremendous loss. The children's loss is even greater, as they are often the most innocent victims of divorce. It is a moral imperative of the highest order for the Church to be concerned for the welfare of the children of divorce. The Church must encourage and admonish divorced parents to do all in their power to provide for the physical, social, cultural, moral and religious upbringing of their children.[50] The community of the faithful should extend pastoral care and love to the children and adults who have suffered from the pain of divorce.

As an aside, a divorced Catholic should not refrain from the reception of holy communion simply because he or she is divorced. It is a common misconception that if Catholics have divorced they have incurred the penalty of excommunication. This is not true. The misunderstanding is probably derived from a Church council held in 1884 that imposed a penalty of excommunication if a Catholic in the United States divorced and then remarried outside of the Church. However, this penalty has ceased to exist.

If an individual believes that his or her marriage is invalid, the Church affords such a divorced person the right to petition for a declaration of nullity.[51] After a wedding has taken place, it is legally presumed that a valid marriage came into existence through the consent of the two parties. A declaration of nullity is a judicial pronouncement that a valid marriage had not been brought about, as the faith community had presumed. The decree focuses either on the presence of a diriment impediment or on a defect of consent in one of the parties or on the celebration of an unauthorized wedding ceremony.

Tribunal investigations are complex and begin with the legal presumption that the marriage in question is indeed valid. Anything to the contrary will have to be proven. The main task of tribunal personnel is to uphold the indissolubility of marriage, not as an ideal, but as a lived reality. Pastoral concern for individuals, no matter how deeply felt, cannot take precedence over the Church's teachings on indissolubility. While individuals have a right to petition the Church for a declaration of nullity, they do not have a right to a declaration of nullity. It is the responsibility of judges to weigh the laws on marriage and the facts of an individual case before coming to a decision.

PART II:

The Public Dimensions
of Marriage

Q. 15. Is marriage solely a private matter between two individuals who love one another?

No.

Some people believe that marriage is purely a private and personal matter—the love of two individuals alone. They ask why the Church involves itself. The answer is that though marriage is indeed personal, it is anything but private. The Church (like the State) considers marriage to be a public act, not simply a private matter between two individuals.

The public dimensions of marriage are attested to on many levels, including the ecclesial and the civil. For instance, both the Church and State place premarital requirements on the bride and groom. Legal qualifications such as a minimum age are also required by both societies. In most states, without a civil license and officiant, there is no civil recognition of marriage. Similarly, two Catholics must marry in the presence of an authorized priest or deacon and two witnesses. If they do not, the Church does not recognize the existence of a marriage.

Civilly, if a person is already married, he or she cannot marry another; to do so is bigamous, and the second marriage is not recognized as valid by the State. Similarly, an individual who is already married cannot marry another person in the Church. He or she is incapable of doing so because of the prior marriage.

These requirements and specifications are but a few examples that demonstrate the public nature of marriage. They underscore the public ramifications of marriage in the Church, including the well-being of the spouses, the welfare of children and the cohesive nature of the community as a whole. As the *Catechism of the Catholic Church* states: "The well-being of the individual person and of both human and Christian society is closely bound up with the healthy state of conjugal and family life."[52] The family is a microcosm of the larger community of the faithful and thus referred to as the "domestic church."

Q. 16. What are the scriptural foundations of marriage?

Marriage is a holy reality established by the Creator. In the creation narratives of the Old Testament, the first human beings appear in this sacred context. They are part of the universe that has been created by God. In the book of Genesis, chapter 1, verse 27, we read: "So God created man in his own image, in the divine image he created him; male and female he created them...." As equals to one another, they participated in the order of creation: "God blessed them, saying, 'Be fertile and multiply: fill the earth and subdue it. Have dominion over the fish of the sea, and the birds of the air, and all the living things that move on the earth'" (Gn 1:28).

The Old Testament describes the marital beliefs and practices of the Hebrews as they lived out their faith. There are personal references to marital unions, for example, that of Abraham and Sarah. There are also references to the institutional aspects of marriage and the family. For instance, to have children in abundance was a great blessing, and the family was considered the primary source of strength for the community at large. Marriage also reflected theological realities. It expressed Yahweh's relationship with Israel. As the human couple lived in a sacred universe, their relationship mirrored the sacred relationship between God and Israel. He was the bridegroom, Israel the bride.

Unlike the Old Testament, the New Testament does not offer a systematic treatment of marriage. Rather, significant references to marriage are found in the Gospels and in some of the Pauline writings. As divorce is problematic today, so too it was problematic in Our Lord's lifetime. Gospel references to the Lord's treatment of divorce are Matthew 5:31–32; Matthew 19:3–9; Mark 10:2–12 and Luke 16:18. Jesus' teachings on the matter are best expressed in Matthew 19:6, when he refers back to the creation verses of the Old Testament: "Thus they are no longer two but one flesh. Therefore let no man separate what God has joined."

However, Jesus' references to marriage are not concerned solely with the problem of divorce. He honored marriage when he performed his first miracle at the wedding feast of Cana. He also used symbolism from marriage, referring to himself as the groom: "Can you make guests of the groom fast while the groom is still with them?" (Lk 5:34).

The writings of St. Paul take the reference of Christ as a groom one step further. Marriage becomes the symbol of the relationship between Christ and his Church: "Husbands, love your wives, as Christ loved the Church. He gave himself up for her....He who loves his wife loves himself....For this reason a man shall leave his father and mother, and shall cling to his wife, and the two shall be made into one" (Eph 5:22–32). St. Paul also demonstrates that divorce remained an unacceptable solution to marital difficulties in the early Christian community (1 Cor 7:10–11; Rom 7:3). The writings of St. Paul also indicate that marriage is not only good for the ordering of the faith community, but it can also be a source of sanctification, even for the unbeliever. We read in 1 Corinthians 7:14: "The unbelieving husband is consecrated by his believing wife; the unbelieving wife is consecrated by her believing husband."

Thus, the New Testament understanding of marriage moves its horizons beyond the Old Testament. Marriage is seen not only as part of the sacred universe, but also in the context of Christ's relationship with his Church. Christians married "in the Lord," and as such, marriage symbolized the old and new covenants.

Q. 17. What are some key historical developments in the Church's teaching on marriage?

The faith community's understanding of marriage is steeped in two thousand years of its lived experience of marriage and theological reflection upon it. Clearly, the theology of marriage has developed over the centuries through a broadening of horizons. Yet, there is no "new" theology of marriage any more than there is a "new" theology of the eucharist. Rather, there have been significant historical developments, with notable shifts in emphases. None of these developments negates or destroys the past. Instead, they build on it, complement it and enrich it. Each age has added its own emphasis.

In the first three centuries the marriages of Christians were not legislated in any official manner. Couples married according to the customs of the place where they lived. The Church addressed pastoral concerns, such as Christians marrying unbelievers and the problem of parents choosing their children's marriage partner, but there was no legislative resolution to these matters. However, the early Christians were concerned about the excesses of the pagan world around them. So some writers began to exalt virginity and abstinence as a backlash against the sexually permissive culture. Unfortunately, this led to a devaluation of marriage due to its sexual component. Marriage began to be viewed as a lesser state in life for those who desired true spiritual enlightenment.

The fourth and fifth centuries witnessed legislation from local Church councils that addressed pastoral problems associated with marriage. Impediments to marriage were established and so some individuals were prohibited from marriage. Laws were also promulgated to restrain marriages of Christians to heretics and unbelievers. In addition, the beginning elements of a marriage liturgy appeared in these centuries—for example, a priest was asked to bless the marriage, rather than the father of the bride.

It is also during this time that St. Augustine (354–430) worked out a systematic treatment of marriage. His teachings have inspired and dominated the development of marriage to the present. Again, since virginity and abstinence were exalted, some justification for marriage was necessary, since it involved the sexual act. Augustine taught that the inherent dangers regarding sex were to be compensated by the immanent "goods" of marriage: children, fidelity and a sacred lifelong commitment. These goods remain part of the Church's teaching on marriage today.

From the fifth century to the tenth century, the ecclesial dimension of marriage was stressed; for example, Pope Leo the Great (440–461) insisted that marriage be celebrated publicly. Theological debate questioned what actually "made" a marriage: consent, the blessing of the Church or consummation. This debate continued over the next seven hundred years, and certain resolutions from these canonical and theological disputations affect us today with regard to the following points: matters concerning the consent of the parties; the manner in which consent is expressed; the legal qualifications of the ministers; and the importance of consummation.

In the twelfth century marriage became synonymous with the concept of "contract." It brought about legal relationships and became explainable in juridical categories. Theoretical expositions on marriage also became more focused at this time. Gratian, a Camaldolese monk and canon lawyer, defended the theory that consent alone between the parties was not enough for marriage to come into existence; sexual intercourse between the spouses was necessary as well. Consent made marriage in a fragile way and consummation made it indissoluble. By the end of the twelfth century, the magisterial writings of Popes Alexander III and Innocent III confirmed that after a marriage had been consummated, it could never be dissolved. This definition of indissolubility remains solid in Church teaching today.

By the end of the twelfth century and into the thirteenth, through the recovery of Greek philosophy, primarily that of Aristotle, new theological systems arose. They are best expressed in the writings of St. Thomas Aquinas (1225–74). Appropriating the Aristotelian worldview that sexuality in itself was good, Aquinas taught that marriage was entirely good and that the act of generation was not sinful. St. Thomas identified the ends of marriage as the procreation of children and the mutual love of the spouses. He also defined consent as the act of one's will under the guidance of the intellect. This philosophical concept is employed constantly in Church courts today.

The sixteenth century brought us the Council of Trent versus the Reformers. The Council defines marriage between the baptized in the most sacred sense: it is one of the seven sacraments. In order to combat secret marriages, the Council imposed the requirement of the "canonical form" on all marriages. So, for validity, marriages had to be performed in the presence of a priest and two witnesses. The implications of this form of marriage are present in today's courts, with declarations of nullity based on a defect of the requisite form. The sixteenth century to the mid-twentieth centuries witnessed further expositions of marriage as a sacrament; marriage as a contract; and marriage with canonical requirements pertaining to validity.

The Second Vatican Council (1962–65) broadened the conceptual nature of marriage as a contract to a fuller appreciation of the sacrament of marriage as a covenant relationship between the spouses and God. Mutual love, the equality of the parties, the call to holiness in marriage were also more deeply formulated. Twenty years after the Council these concepts were incorporated into the 1983 Code of Canon Law.

Q. 18. What are the central theological elements of marriage in Church teaching today?

Our present understanding of marriage is the sum total of all that has come before us. The principal purpose of the Second Vatican Council was to enter into dialogue with the world in a language that was understandable to people. The dignity of the human person and the role of the human person in the world—specifically in marriage and family life—were of deep pastoral concern. With this focus, the council fathers decided to describe marriage as "an intimate community of conjugal life and love" in the conciliar document *The Pastoral Constitution on the Church in the Modern World* (no. 48).

The description of marriage as "an intimate community of conjugal life and love" has deep biblical connotations insofar as it underscores Genesis 2:24 and Matthew 19:6 that "the two become one flesh." This "intimate community" is by its nature ordered to the good of the spouses and the procreation and education of children. Furthermore, as a sacrament, marriage enjoys a special dignity, since through it Christian spouses encounter Jesus in an intimate fashion. All of these elements and others were then diligently incorporated into the 1983 Code of Canon Law.[53]

The central elements of marriage define it as a covenant, a partnership and, when between two baptized persons, a sacrament. The purpose of every marriage is the good of the spouses and the procreation and education of children. These principles find legal expression in canon 1055.1:

> The matrimonial covenant by which a man and a woman
> establish between themselves a partnership of the whole
> of life, is by its nature ordered toward the good of the
> spouses and procreation and education of offspring; this
> covenant between baptized persons has been raised by
> Christ the Lord to the dignity of a sacrament.

This legal description of marriage is key, for once the Church states what marriage is, it also has set the parameters for what marriage is not. The union of a man and a woman that is devoid of any one of these central elements cannot in essence be marriage.

Q. 19. What is the marital covenant?

The *Catechism of the Catholic Church* states: "The intimate community of life and love which constitutes the married state has been established by the Creator and endowed by him with its own proper laws....God himself is the author of marriage."[54] In this sense, marriage transcends the individuals. It is an institution through which they live out their call to holiness, that is, their call to life in communion with God.

Marriage is a reality that has been instituted by God. It is a covenant relationship, that is both private and public: *private* in the sense that it is a personal bond, or covenant of love; *public* insofar as it establishes legal rights and obligations for the parties, and because it affects the whole community of believers.

In the past marriage was defined primarily as a contract with private and public implications. However, this definition is deficient, as it suggests marriage is arbitrarily placed by the will of the individuals who embrace it, and therefore its disposal can be left to them. Furthermore, the word *contract* is deficient in regard to the divine aspects of marriage.

It is interesting to note that the fathers of the Second Vatican Council never used the word contract when discussing marriage in *The Pastoral Constitution on the Church in the Modern World* (articles 47–52). They were insistent that the biblical word *covenant* be used instead. It is in article 47 of the constitution that a working description of marriage as covenant is found:

> ...[it is] an intimate partnership of life and love established by the Creator and qualified by His laws, rooted in the conjugal covenant of irrevocable personal consent.

In the past we have understood marriage to be a contract whose object was the transfer of rights for procreative acts. The primary end of marriage was procreation. However, what is being said now is that marriage is a covenant. The word *covenant* does not deny the contractual dimension of marriage, as there is not an either/or approach to marriage. Marriage is both contract and covenant. However, by highlighting marriage as covenant, the limitations of marriage as contract are balanced. Within the covenant the spouses express their love under God's grace, and they order their love to God's gift of children.

Q. 20. What is the sacrament of marriage?

Marriage between the baptized has been raised by Christ himself to the dignity of a sacrament.[55] It is a sign of God's covenant with humanity. Marriage is fundamentally related to the saving work of Jesus Christ. Christians believe that salvation is God's communication of himself as love; it is the divine and unconditional acceptance of humanity in all of its strengths and weaknesses. When humanity accepts God in return through love, the work of salvation is established. The union of husband and wife is an effective sign of this reality.

In the Old Testament God established a covenant of love with his people, Israel. Marriage was an expressive sign and symbol of this covenant. Jesus is the most unique and definitive expression of divine love insofar as he is the communication of divinity to humanity. Through Jesus, God has accepted, affirmed and redeemed humanity. This is why Christian marriage takes on a new meaning beyond that of a good and natural marriage. When a baptized man and a woman marry in Christ, their love is purified and fulfilled by God. A Christian marriage is not simply a sign and symbol of divine love. Rather, it is an effective sign, a fulfilled symbol and a real manifestation of the love of God as revealed in Jesus Christ.

When a Christian bride and groom marry, they invite God into their covenantal union of love. The sacramentality of marriage rests on this covenant of love between two people, a union that both reflects and shares in divine love. A married love makes present to the world Christ's union of love with his Church; it is in this graced, sacramental union that a family comes into being.

The reality of sacramental love is summed up beautifully in *The Pastoral Constitution on the Church in the Modern World* (nos. 47–50):

> Thus, a man and woman, who by the marriage covenant of conjugal love...render mutual help and service to each other through an intimate union of their persons...Christ the Lord abundantly blessed this many-faceted love, welling up as it does from the foundation of divine love and structured as it is on the model of His union with the Church. For as God of old made himself present to His people through a covenant of love and fidelity....Authentic married love is caught up into divine love and is governed and enriched by Christ's redeeming power...this love is an eminently human one since it is directed from one person to another through an affection of the will. It involves the good of the whole person....This love is uniquely expressed and perfected through the marital act....Marriage and conjugal love are by their nature ordained toward the begetting and education of children....

Q. 21. How is God's grace operative in the "sacred bond" of marriage?

The sacred bond of marriage is not a separate reality existing above or alongside the couple. A wedding ceremony does not bring about a magical entity that exists beyond the parties. Rather, the bond of faithfulness expressed between husband and wife has a religious dimension. God is invited into the union of their love. Thus, an unbreakable bond of unity is established between the parties and God.

God's grace is present both in Christian marriages and in good and natural marriages. As God himself is the author of marriage, he blesses good and natural marriage. In the Old Testament this form of marriage modeled the covenant of love between God and his people Israel. When a man and a woman have truly consented in love to live God's intended institution of marriage, he is present to them. Good and natural marriages are ordered toward the good of the spouses and the procreation and education of children. The three goods of marriage—children, fidelity and a sacred lifelong commitment—are basic to the union. The essential properties of a good and natural marriage are unity and indissolubility, though this latter property is not as firmly established in a good and natural marriage as it is in a Christian marriage.

God's presence in a Christian marriage moves beyond that of a good and natural marriage. In this instance two baptized individuals marry in the Lord. They thereby participate in Christ's sanctifying service. Their marriage is not a symbol of Christ's union with the Church; rather, it is one with that union. To say that marriage is a sacrament is to say that it is an outward, visible, tangible sign of an inner, invisible reality. It is a sign of Christ's love for his Church. The marital love of a husband and wife is a sign that makes present to the world God's love and faithfulness.

Sacraments are effective signs. This means that they bring about, effect and confer what they signify. In sacraments, by the power of the Holy Spirit, the real presence of God comes into the world. So, for example, at mass, through the power of the Holy Spirit, bread and wine become the real presence of Christ—body, blood, soul and divinity. Through the waters of baptism a person is filled with the Holy Spirit. In marriage a husband and wife choose to take each other in good times and in bad, in sickness and in health until death. Through their free and personal act of the will partners surrender themselves to each other in a lifelong sacred commitment that is imbued with God's sanctifying grace.

Q. 22. If love dies, does the sacrament cease?

No.

As previously indicated, the conciliar document, *The Pastoral Constitution on the Church in the Modern World*, placed a great deal of emphasis on the importance of conjugal love. The word *love* appears twenty-eight times in articles 48 and 49 alone. This concept of conjugal love was not easily arrived at during the council, for it presented problems for many of the council fathers. There was a concern that marriages could be terminated when love died if they placed too much emphasis on the word *love*.

Yet, the council fathers made it quite clear that they mean much more than emotional love or romance when placing the word in the context of marriage. They are concerned with the commitment involved in mutual love. This is a selfless love that mirrors Christ's own sacrificial love. In matrimony, one consents to an acceptance of marriage as a community of love. If this love does become extinct, then it becomes the duty of the partners to do everything in their power to rekindle it.

This is aptly expressed in an opening prayer of the nuptial mass:

Father, you have made the bond of marriage a holy mystery, a symbol of Christ's love for his Church. Hear our prayers today for this groom and bride. With faith in you and in each other they pledge their love today. May their lives always bear witness to the reality of that love. We ask this through Christ Our Lord. Amen.

Q. 23. Is the priest the minister of Christian marriage?

No.

It is crucial to keep in mind that the bride and the groom are the ministers of the sacrament of marriage. The man gives the sacrament to the woman, and the woman gives the sacrament to the man under the light of grace. As the *Catechism of the Catholic Church* states: "In the Latin Church, it is ordinarily understood that the spouses, as ministers of God's grace, mutually confer upon each other the Sacrament of Matrimony by expressing their consent before the Church."[56] The Church teaches that it is the consent of the two ministers that brings about the sacrament of marriage.

In spite of this theological tenet, most people think that the priest or deacon is the minister of the sacrament. He is often called the "minister," but this is incorrect. Rather, he is an "official" witness of the Church. Along with the best man and maid of honor, he is one of three individuals who witness what the two ministers are doing.

This confusion is understandable because usually the priest or deacon is the minister of a sacrament. In addition, the wedding ritual implicitly suggests that he is the minister. For instance, during the wedding ceremony the priest extends his arm in blessing over the couple. This liturgical action of blessing is often misconstrued as the moment the sacrament is conferred. However, this is not the moment of conferral. The sacrament comes about when the bride and groom exchange their vows. As soon as the exchange of vows has happened, the sacrament has come into existence. The priest's liturgical gesture is a blessing of this sacramental act of the couple.

Q. 24. How does marriage come into existence legally?

Remembering that the ministers of marriage are the bride and the groom, the law declares that marriage is brought about through: (1) the consent of the bride and groom, (2) legitimately manifested, (3) by those qualified according to the law (again, the bride and the groom).[57] When a wedding takes place, it is legally presumed that a marriage has come into existence

However, if the consent of the bride and groom was defective, in one or both of the parties, then marriage was NOT brought about. If their consent was NOT legitimately manifested, then marriage was NOT brought about. If either the bride or the groom was unqualified by law to place consent, then marriage was NOT brought about. An ecclesiastical declaration of nullity decrees that for a particular reason a marriage had not come into existence on the wedding day, as everyone had presumed.

Q. 25. What is meant by the expression, "marriage enjoys the favor of the law"?

Whenever anyone questions the validity of a marriage—whether Christian or good and natural—the legal norm invoked is that marriage enjoys the "favor of the law."[58] The law presumes that the marriage in question is valid, so anything to the contrary will have to be proven. Nevertheless, like any legal presumption in any legal system, it is a "presumption." It will yield to contrary evidence. Analogously, in American criminal law, a well-known legal presumption is that you are innocent until you are proven to be guilty.

The presumption is innocence. Yet, if enough proof is brought forward to indicate otherwise, the presumption of innocence will yield to the verdict of guilt.

In much the same way, in Church law any marriage that takes place is legally presumed to be a valid marriage. As with most legal presumptions this one upholds a basic purpose of the law, which is to provide stability for the community. In regard to marriage, if a doubt (no matter how reasonable) could extinguish the lifelong sacred commitment of marriage, the community would be most unstable.

The law values truth above all else. If a doubt regarding the validity of a marriage is serious, truth demands an investigation. If evidence exists to corroborate the doubt, then the presumption of validity will yield to a declaration of nullity. Tribunal investigations focus on the parties' consent, the legitimate manifestation of their consent and the parties' legal qualifications to place consent.

Q. 26. Can a nonconsummated marriage be dissolved by the Church?

Yes.

The Church holds that a valid marriage between two baptized Christians which is consummated is absolutely indissoluble.[59] It cannot be dissolved by the will of the couple or any human agency—civil or Church. Only death dissolves the union. So, conversely, a nonconsummated marriage is dissoluble. It can be dissolved. The theological basis for this is found in the twelfth-century debate on what makes marriage—consent or consummation. Some held that consent alone between the parties brought about marriage; others contended that sexual intercourse between the spouses brought about marriage. The resolution was that consent made marriage and consummation made it indissoluble. This understanding of indissolubility remains Church teaching today.

The law presumes consumption after the spouses begin living together.[60] However, the Holy Father, for a just cause, at the request of one or both of the parties, may dissolve a valid Christian marriage if it can be proven that the marriage was not consummated. He will also dissolve a valid good and natural marriage that was not consummated.[61] In both instances substantial proof overturns the legal presumption that the marriage had been consummated.

There are specific legal procedures to be followed in these cases.[62] Initially the local tribunal puts the case together and then forwards it to the Vatican. Ultimately, the pope alone judges the case. The present procedures respect the personal dignity of both parties. These cases are processed with a great deal of discretion and tact; they are, in fact, relatively rare.

Q. 27. Can a good and natural marriage be dissolved by the Church?

Yes.

A marriage is sacramental if both of the parties are baptized Christians.[63] So conversely, if one or both of the parties is not baptized, the marriage is nonsacramental. It is considered a good and natural marriage and thus valid in Church law; by virtue of their consent the parties have brought about the union of husband and wife. This union is blessed by God, whether it is between Muslims, Jews, Hindus or Buddhists. So if a Jewish man marries a Jewish woman in the presence of the rabbi, the Catholic Church considers that to be a valid good and natural marriage.

One of the essential properties of every marriage (Christian and good and natural) is indissolubility—the parties are bound to the commitment for life. However, indissolubility admits to gradations. In a Christian marriage the property of indissolubility acquires a "distinctive firmness by reason of the sacrament."[64] The Church holds that a valid marriage between two baptized Christians that is consummated is absolutely indissoluble.[65] It cannot be dissolved by the will of the couple or by any human agency—civil or Church. Only death dissolves the union.

A good and natural marriage is indissoluble as well, but in this case indissolubility is not absolute. Though the good and natural marriage cannot be dissolved by the will of the parties or the agency of the State, in certain circumstances it can be dissolved by the Church. The reason for the dissolution is always based on an individual's ability to practice Christianity.

There are two processes in Church law that dissolve good and natural marriages: the Pauline privilege and the favor of the faith. The former is supervised by the bishop. It is rooted in the New Testament account of St. Paul (1 Cor 7:12–15):

> If any brother has a wife who is an unbeliever but is willing to live with him, he must not divorce her. And if any woman has a husband who is an unbeliever but is willing to live with her, she must not divorce him....If the unbeliever wishes to separate, however, let him do so. The believing husband and wife is not bound in such cases.

The Church's present application of the Pauline privilege has discernible roots in the process that addressed a serious pastoral issue in the sixteenth century Church. Missionaries had to contend with the problem of polygamous marriages among converts to Christianity in West and South India, the Antilles, a large portion of South America and the Philippine Islands. How could converts live out their newfound Christianity if they had multiple marriage partners? How were the missionaries to deal with good and natural marriages versus Christian marriages? There was the need to strengthen the faith of the newly baptized. What was to be done regarding proper support for the children and wives of multiple unions? Recourse to the Pauline privilege addressed these pastoral dilemmas.

As then, so now, this privilege concerns a marriage between two unbaptized persons with the subsequent desire of conversion for one of the parties. When one of the parties to a good and natural marriage receives baptism **and** the other party leaves the marriage with no intention of returning, the Pauline privilege may be invoked. The good and natural marriage is dissolved when the party who has been baptized contracts a new marriage.[66]

The Pauline privilege could be applied to a case involving two divorced Hindus. Though divorced both are bound to their good and natural marriage in the eyes of the Church. The essential element of indissolubility means it cannot be dissolved by their wills or any action of the State. If, however, the Hindu man becomes a baptized Catholic and wishes to marry a Catholic in the Church, he may be allowed to do so through the Pauline privilege. The new Christian marriage dissolves the prior good and natural marriage.

The second procedure that dissolves a good and natural marriage is referred to as a "favor of the faith." As the missionary Church confronted the pastoral issue of polygamous marriages in the sixteenth century, the twentieth century brought about a new pastoral concern in regard to good and natural marriages. Frequent marriages between the baptized and the unbaptized, the spread of divorce and the desire of divorced persons to marry in the Church led to the implementation of the favor of the faith procedure.

This procedure involves the good and natural marriage of two unbaptized persons or the good and natural marriage of a baptized person and a nonbaptized person. In this instance the pope dissolves the good and natural marriage in **favor of the Christian faith** when one of the parties of that marriage has either become a Catholic or wishes to marry a Catholic.

Take the case of a Lutheran and a Buddhist who marry

and divorce. Both are bound to this good and natural marriage in the eyes of the Church. As time passes, suppose a single Catholic man falls in love and wishes to marry the divorced Lutheran woman. He is unable to do so because of her prior bond. An acceptable pastoral response to this dilemma is for her to petition the pope to dissolve her good and natural marriage in "favor" of the faith of her Catholic fiancé. The underlying principle of the favor of the faith is the Catholic's ability to practice the faith.

PART III:

The Diamond of Consent

Q. 28. What is consent?

The law declares that marriage is brought about through: (1) the consent of the bride and groom, (2) legitimately manifested, (3) by those qualified according to the law (again, the bride and the groom).[67] So, if the consent of the party(ies) was defective, then marriage was NOT brought about.

Consent is an "act of the will." This is a philosophical concept that is difficult to grasp. Yet, the parties manifest what their wills desire when they say "I do" or repeat the marriage vows. As the *Catechism of the Catholic Church* states: "The Church holds the exchange of consent between the spouses to be the indispensable element that 'makes the marriage.' If consent is lacking there is no marriage."[68]

The law presumes a person is **ready, able** and **willing** to place the act of the will that brings about marriage. Thus the act is multifaceted; a visual comparison to the act's many facets is the wedding diamond. The essential components of this act are described negatively in law, insofar as the law defines when the wedding vows are defective.[69]

A person is **ready** for marriage if one has the required knowledge. A person must know that marriage entails a permanent partnership ordered toward the procreation of children. If one is ignorant of this, then consent is defective and the marriage is invalid.[70] One must also have a knowledge of whom he or she is marrying. If one is in error regarding the person, then there is no valid marriage. Obviously, if a person marries the wrong identical twin, the marriage is invalid. Or, if one is in error regarding an intended specified "quality" in the person, consent is invalid.[71] Finally, the knowledge required for marriage to this particular person must be based on truth. If deceit or fraud is involved, the consent is invalid.[72]

A person must be **able** to marry, that is, he or she must have the capacity for placing an act of the will. A person who lacks the use of reason is not able to give valid consent and thus bring about a marriage.[73] So a thirty-year-old with the intelligence quotient of a five-year-old is incapable of consent because this person lacks the intelligence necessary to carry out the obligations of marriage. A person is also rendered incapable of marriage if he or she suffers from a grave lack of discretion of judgment on the wedding day.[74] For instance, an alcoholic who has been raised in a physically abusive and alcoholic home may become entrapped in a physically abusive and drug-dependent relationship that leads to a wedding. A person trapped in this cycle of violence, chemical abuse and dependency is incapable of exercising the requisite judgment concerning the essential rights and obligations that are to be mutually given and accepted in marriage. The person's consent may be invalid. Finally, a person is incapable of contracting marriage if he or she is unable to assume the essential obligations of marriage due to psychological reasons.[75] So, for example, a person untreated for multiple personality disorders might marry invalidly.

Finally, when persons marry they **will** to bring about the sacred bond of marriage, whether they enter into a Christian marriage or a good and natural marriage. If any of the essential elements of marriage, or marriage itself, is excluded on the day of the wedding, the consent of the party(ies) is defective and the marriage invalid. So if any of the three goods identified by St. Augustine are excluded from consent (children, fidelity or perpetuity), or the entire marriage covenant is excluded, then there was a wedding, but no marriage was brought about on the wedding day.[76] In addition, the act of the will may not place any future conditions on marriage; if so, there is invalidity.[77] Lastly, the act of consent must be free. If it is forced or there is an inordinate amount of fear influencing the will of the party(ies), then again, the marriage was invalid from its beginning.[78]

Q. 29. What is the legal theory behind a declaration of nullity based on defective consent?

The ministers' consent on the wedding day is like the wedding diamond insofar as it is multifaceted. As outlined in the previous answer, their consent is a free act of the will, not a forced act. There must be an understanding of what marriage is all about with its essential elements of perpetuity, fidelity and conjugal love, which is open to children. Basically, it is presumed that the ministers marry according to the teachings of the Church.

It is required that there be good discretionary judgment on the part of both parties as they consent to the marriage. In other words, there are no red flags raised that signal to the individuals, "Don't get married at this point in your life"; "Don't marry this particular person"; "Don't marry; this relationship is seriously troubled"; and so forth. It is presumed that neither party suffers from an untreated grave psychological illness. There is no fraud. There are no conditions placed on consent. There is no error about an essential quality of the person one is about to marry, or an error in regard to the actual person. There is a willingness and capacity to fulfill the obligations of marriage. All of these facets of consent and other relevant considerations are presumed to be healthy and active in the ministers.

Tribunal proceedings regarding nullity attempt to determine if any facet of the diamond of consent was defective in one or both of the parties on the wedding day. The presumption is that everything required for a valid union was indeed present. The burden of proof to the contrary is on the one petitioning the Church for the declaration of nullity. A tribunal can declare only whether or not it has been proven that a marriage was invalid from the start.

Any individual has the right to petition the Church for a declaration of nullity;[79] this is very different from saying that one has a right to a declaration of nullity; no one has such a right. However, if it can be proven that something essential was lacking in the consent of one or both of the parties on the wedding day, the Church will grant the declaration of nullity.

Q. 30. How are cases decided?

If a person believes his or her marriage to be invalid, that person may petition a Church court to undertake a tribunal investigation regarding nullity. The validity of a marriage is challenged by the formulation of a doubt. This doubt determines the ground, or grounds, on which the marriage is alleged to be invalid.[80] The law lists various grounds and defines them very precisely.[81]

The ensuing trial investigates whether the marriage is null on the grounds that have been established. For instance, the validity of a marriage may be questioned on the grounds of force or grave fear. The parties are notified that these are the grounds upon which the case will be investigated. The testimonies of the parties, witnesses and perhaps experts from various disciplines will be evaluated in view of these grounds. Ultimately, the final sentence of the judges will answer the doubt as to whether or not the marriage is invalid because force or grave fear was present on the wedding day.

Since every marriage is unique, the application of the law will be applied uniquely to each case. Judges evaluate the circumstances of a case in light of the grounds upon which the petition is based. The laws that list the grounds are succinct and precise, so more is required for a proper evaluation. Judges turn to supplementary sources of law, in particular to jurisprudence. *Jurisprudence* could be defined as the application of the law in a particular case. It is a body of case law gleaned from the decisions of higher courts. When judges of lower courts apply the law to a case, they turn to the jurisprudence and practice of the central organizations of the Holy See (the Vatican).[82]

In judicial matters, the Roman Rota is the highest court of appeal in the Church. It often deals with marriage nullity cases. The Apostolic Signatura is the highest supervisory court in the Church.[83] It is concerned with the proper application and implementation of law throughout the worldwide Church. The application of the law by these two courts is the legal guide used by judges throughout the world when determining the invalidity of a marriage and the proper implementation of trial procedures.

The judges of the Roman Rota publish their judicial sentences in cases that have been decided either in the affirmative or in the negative. The sentence states the grounds upon which the case was presented. It then argues the case in light of the law and the case facts. The sentence clearly indicates why the decision is affirmative or negative in view of the collected testimonies. These sentences are invaluable legal sources to judges around the world. The decisions of rotal judges are cited in the decisions of lower court judges. In fact, rotal decisions are crucial to the judicial life of the Church, as they are one of the primary sources of jurisprudence for the worldwide Church.

Q. 31. What is lack of due reason?

A person must be **able** to marry. One is rendered incapable of marriage if one lacks a sufficient use of reason.[84] Clearly, if a person does not have the use of reason, he or she cannot know what marriage is or understand its obligations. It is not that a person is intellectually mistaken in regard to marriage, but rather, is fundamentally lacking the ability to comprehend.

This inability to know may be permanent and rooted in a severe mental handicap or brain damage. For example, an individual with an intelligence quotient of a five-year-old may be prompted to say, "I do" at a wedding ceremony, but the words are meaningless—both to the individual and in law. Though a wedding ceremony may have taken place, there was no valid marriage. The lack of a sufficient use of due reason may also be temporary—for example, if caused by drug use. Suppose the groom ingested LSD prior to the ceremony. He is temporarily rendered incapable of consent, as he lacked the faculty of reason at the moment he exchanged consent. There was a wedding ceremony, but the marriage was invalid from its beginning.

Q. 32. What is a grave lack of discretion of judgment?

A person must be **able** to marry. One is incapable of contracting marriage if one suffers from a grave lack of discretion of judgment concerning the essential matrimonial rights and obligations to be mutually given and accepted.[85] Now this is **not** the same as age-appropriate immaturity or premarital jitters. The law presumes that every person is capable of consenting to marriage. The act of the will required for marriage is not an unattainable ideal or act of heroism! It is an act performed by millions of persons annually.

Nonetheless, the law admits that some persons are incapable of contracting marriage due to a **grave** lack of discretion of judgment. The more important the decision, the more that is required of a person's capacity for appropriate judgment. A decision to marry another person for life requires mature powers of judgment. A person's powers of judgment rest on his or her knowledge, experience and maturity. A fifteen-year-old American child prodigy may "know" all about marriage, but that child "knows" little about life. Hence, the child suffers from a grave discretion of judgment if he or she consents to marriage.

Since the law stipulates that the lack of discretion must be grave, the person's powers of judgment must be removed completely or be so clouded by external factors that the person is incapable of consent. When evaluating this defect of consent, the tribunal investigation is not confined to the wedding ceremony, but also concerns itself with the entire period of time during which the person decided and consented to marry. Reports from psychological or psychiatric experts are often required. Testimonies from the parties to the marriage and witnesses are also utilized to substantiate this ground.

A CASE: Tom and Mary marry at age twenty-one. Tom had a tough childhood and adolescence. He was abandoned at birth and raised in six foster homes until age eighteen. Not one of the foster homes provided stability or love to Tom. In fact, he was sexually abused from ages seven through ten while living in the third home. He never spoke of the abuse to anyone. He began drinking at twelve and became a habitual user of pot by fourteen. He dropped out of high school at seventeen. He had seven jobs from ages sixteen to twenty-one. Mary came into his life in January. She was his first serious girlfriend. They became sexually active within two weeks. They became engaged and married within six months.

The marriage lasted three years and one child was born. Tom drank a lot and smoked pot daily, but Mary loved him.

One day Tom just walked out because he was unhappy. After having seen Tom only twice in three years, Mary divorced him. During this interim, Tom has had nothing to do with his daughter, and Mary is certain he is still floating through life on alcohol, pot and multiple unemployments. She ultimately petitioned the court for a declaration of nullity based on the grounds of Tom's grave lack of discretion of judgment when they married.

It is not too difficult to prove the nullity of Tom and Mary's marriage from the facts as cited in the testimonies of witnesses. The judges would also gather further evidence from experts in the field of the behavioral sciences regarding child abandonment issues, child sexual abuse and chemical dependencies. Taking into consideration the law, rotal jurisprudence and the facts, the case would most likely be decided in the affirmative. Tom would be considered incapable of contracting marriage on the wedding day, as he suffered from a grave lack of discretion of judgment concerning the essential rights and obligations of marriage. While there certainly had been a wedding, the marriage was invalid from its beginning.

Q. 33. What does it mean to declare a marriage null on the ground of a lack of due competence?

A person must be **able** to marry. A psychologically healthy person is capable of assuming the ordinary obligations of marriage. Conversely, one is incapable of contracting marriage if one is unable to assume the essential obligations of marriage because of "causes of a psychological nature."[86] This is sometimes called a lack of due competence in law. Therefore, if a person suffers from a serious untreated psychological illness, he or she may not be capable of assuming these obligations.

Church law does not list the essential obligations of marriage in detail. Neither does developing jurisprudence present an exhaustive listing. In addition, since the behavioral sciences are still developing, the "causes of a psychological nature" that render one incapable of marriage are not set in stone. Nonetheless, they are considered serious causes and reside in the psychological constitution of the person. It's not enough for individuals to suggest that they felt unloved as children and thereby propose themselves to have been incapable of marriage on this ground. Rather, there must be a serious psychological defect that was present on the wedding day. It is often necessary for experts in the field of psychology to serve as witnesses in cases based on this ground.

A judge considering nullity on these grounds examines the behavior of the person before and after consent. If it is proven that a person could not fulfill the basic obligations of marriage because of a psychological illness, the judge concludes in favor of nullity on the ground of a lack of due competence. Certainly one cannot assume the responsibility for what one cannot fulfill.

Experts in the field of psychology have identified serious psychological illnesses such as schizophrenia and paranoia. They have also identified personality disorders, including antisocial, borderline, histrionic and narcissistic disorders. It is important to note that the presence of these illnesses does not necessarily constitute defective consent. Individuals under treatment for their illness may indeed be quite capable of assuming the obligations of marriage. However, when untreated, psychological factors can render a person incapable of marriage on the wedding day.

A CASE: Angela thought Peter was just quiet by nature. Sure, during the two-year courtship he depended on her and had no friends of his own, but she was enamored of his possessiveness. She found it endearing. Soon after the wedding, however, these endearing traits became ominous. He constantly questioned her whereabouts. He was convinced that she was constantly deceiving him, but there was no basis for his mistrust. He constantly read hidden meanings into her innocent remarks. He soon became violent, both emotionally and physically. She began to fear for her safety. The marriage was over in less than a year. The protracted divorce was a nightmare for Angela because of Peter's threats and bizarre behavior.

Shortly after the divorce became final, Peter suffered a nervous breakdown and was hospitalized. He was diagnosed as paranoid. The experts situated the onset of the illness in his adolescence, though its severe manifestations were not present until after he had married. Angela petitioned the Church for a declaration of nullity and it was granted on the ground of Peter's lack of due competence. In this case the tribunal investigation concluded that Peter was incapable of contracting marriage, since he was unable to assume its essential obligations because he suffered from paranoia. There certainly had been a wedding, but the marriage was invalid from its beginning.

Q. 34. What does it mean when a marriage has been declared null on ignorance?

This ground presumes that a person is able to marry, but questions whether the person is **ready** for marriage. On the day of the wedding a person must possess the requisite knowledge concerning the nature of marriage. He or she must know that marriage is: (1) a permanent partnership (2) which is heterosexual and (3) ordered to the procreation of children through sexual cooperation. If any person lacks this knowledge at the time of consent, that person, then, is ignorant and cannot bring about marriage.[87] The law presumes that such ignorance, the lack of appropriate knowledge, does not exist after puberty.[88]

Ignorance concerning the first two elements of marriage is normally not an issue. Individuals with the use of reason know that marriage is a permanent relationship between a man and a woman. Admittedly, modern influences in Western societies, such as the "divorce mentality" and homosexual unions, may affect a person's understanding of marriage. However, it would be rare that a person is ignorant of these first two elements. The ground of ignorance is more often utilized in regard to a lack of knowledge concerning sexual intercourse. The law states that the parties must not be ignorant of the fact that children are conceived through the act of sexual intercourse.

You may ask, how can any person living in the late twentieth century not be aware of the "facts of life?" Just turn on the TV; go to a movie; read a magazine; surf the Net! It's a good question, and, in fact, the law presumes the same reality. Every teenager who has completed puberty is presumed to have knowledge concerning the nature of sexual intercourse. Yet, like any other legal presumption, it yields to contrary proof.

A CASE: Ignatius and Nora were attracted to one another because both were shy and quiet. Both had been only children and sheltered by their elderly parents. Neither had many friends growing up—no friends, in fact—that's what drew them together. Neither had ever dated anyone else before they met at age twenty. After a six month courtship they married.

Unfortunately, the marriage only lasted four years, with no children, and they divorced. Ignatius remarried civilly two years later. Almost immediately he petitioned the Church for a declaration of nullity from his marriage to Nora. The ground for the case was set as ignorance. After he married civilly, Ignatius had learned about the true nature of "sexual cooperation." In his marriage to Nora, there had never been sexual intercourse. Both Ignatius and Nora testified that on the honeymoon they were uncertain as to the proper technique concerning intercourse. In their ignorance, attempts at penetration in different places "down there" had proved too painful for Nora. So both assumed that any further attempts in that area were not natural, and thus they were avoided.

They knew children were conceived through some form of "sex" and together assumed that this occurred by "topical" insemination. During the four years of marriage, they attempted conception by means of his ejaculation on her abdomen. It was obvious to the court that both parties were ignorant of the fact that marriage is ordered to the procreation of children through sexual intercourse. Due to their ignorance, the tribunal declared that a marriage had not come about on the wedding day, as everyone had presumed.

Q. 35. What does it mean to be in error regarding the "person"?

As stated, a person must be **ready** for marriage. He or she must not only possess the requisite knowledge concerning the nature of marriage, but must also have a knowledge of the person they're marrying. If an individual is in error regarding his or her fiancé, then such a person's consent is invalid.[89] Error differs from ignorance; while ignorance is a lack of due knowledge, error is false judgment, a defect in understanding.

If a marriage is declared invalid on the ground of error of person, then there had been an error regarding the identity of the intended spouse on the wedding day. These cases are extremely rare, but nonetheless feasible. Perhaps the parties have never met before the wedding, as in the case of a mail order spouse, for example. As bizarre as this seems, reports have recently surfaced among nations that Internet marriages of this sort do occur—the present-day version of the "mail order bride" scenario, if you will. Michael from MIT may think he is marrying Philomena from the Philippines. But in fact the fiancée who arrives from this other nation is Iris, the impostor! Michael marries the wrong person; he is in error regarding the identity of his intended.

Another example concerns identical twins. Suppose the unintended twin is substituted for the intended twin on the day of the wedding. The one marrying is in error regarding the person with whom consent has been exchanged. In both instances, the marriage would be declared null based on error regarding the identity of the person.

Though there had been a wedding, the marriage was invalid from its beginning.

Q. 36. What is an error regarding a "quality" of a person?

A person must be **ready** for marriage. He or she must not only possess the requisite knowledge concerning the nature of marriage, but must also have a knowledge of the person they're marrying. If one is in error regarding a specific intended quality in the marriage partner, then his or her consent could be invalid.[90]

The quality in question must be directly and principally intended by the person placing the consent. It is considered to be "directly" intended when the quality is intended in and of itself. It is "principally" intended when the quality is more important than the person. Admittedly, intentionality is a difficult concept to grasp; the issue is often more gray than black and white. The concept is more easily explained this way: if the person had known that the intended quality was not present in the spouse on the wedding day, then he or she would never have married that individual.

A CASE: Heather's parents divorced when she was twelve years old. Her father announced that he was gay and left the family. With the exception of a few holiday visits, he had nothing to do with Heather and her two younger brothers. The children were raised admirably by her mother. Nevertheless, while growing up, Heather was keenly aware of her mother's pain due to the broken marriage and its circumstances.

Heather's life went on, and she dated quite a bit in high school and college. Eventually, she met Bill and knew "he was the one." Though he had not dated as extensively as Heather, he did have a broken engagement from a three-year relationship. However, Heather was unfazed by this, as it had ended two years before they had met. Their relationship was not a rebound. After a two-year courtship and one-year engagement, they married. Their first two children were born within four years of the wedding. However, in the fifth year of marriage, the couple divorced.

Heather had accidentally stumbled upon a secret Bill had kept from most people who knew him. One night she surreptitiously logged onto the Internet under his name and password. When she opened the electronic mail, there, to her horror, were dozens of pornographic messages—from women and men! She was faced with the reality that Bill was bisexual.

When Heather confronted Bill, she discovered that although most of his acting out was over the Net, he had engaged in bisexual activity on a number of occasions during the marriage. Although embarrassed that he was caught, he was also relieved. This was who he was, and he was not going to change. If she didn't like it, she could leave him, as his first fiancée had done! Heather did just that, and soon petitioned the Church for a declaration of nullity.

The marriage was declared null on the ground of error concerning a quality of the person. If Heather had known of Bill's sexual attraction to men, especially in light of her family history, she would never have married him. It was shown in this case that she had principally and directly intended to marry a heterosexual man on the day of her wedding. Since she was in error about Bill's true sexuality, the marriage was declared invalid. There certainly had been a wedding, but the marriage was invalid from its beginning.

Q. 37. What if a person is deceived on the wedding day?

A person must be **ready** for marriage. He or she must not only possess the requisite knowledge concerning the nature of marriage, but must also have a knowledge of the intended spouse. If an individual is deceived by the fiancé, then consent is invalid. Technically, this is called imposed error. It is not the consent of the deceiver that is invalid, but rather the consent of the one deceived. The deceived spouse is in error regarding an intended quality in the other spouse. The error is so serious that, had the individual known about it, he or she would never have married.[91]

The law places a number of qualifications on the nature of the deceit. First, it must be real, not imagined. Second, the person deceiving does so in order to marry. Third, the deceit must concern a "quality" of the party that is so serious in nature that it can seriously disrupt the marriage. There is no list of qualities set forth in the law. However, qualities of such a serious nature would include: possession of a serious medical condition, such as a sexually transmitted disease, psychiatric illness, HIV/AIDS, pregnancy by someone else, a criminal record or an immoral lifestyle. Criteria for these and other qualities would be both objective and subjective in nature.

A CASE: Rich and Abby met when both were twenty-three years old. They dated for five years and married, but the marriage was over in six months. Before meeting Abby, Rich had been very involved in the pro-life movement, at times in a militant manner. He began his pro-life commitment when he was sixteen years old. During the courtship he introduced Abby to the movement. She was moved by Rich's commitment to the unborn. She came to believe in the pro-life movement as strongly as he did. During the last two years of the courtship she attended rallies and sit-ins with him. Everyone who knew the couple was inspired by their commitment.

Unfortunately, Abby had a secret. She had become pregnant at age eighteen and had had an abortion. She deeply regretted her action at the time, knowing it was wrong. Shortly after the abortion she had confessed her sin with true contrition. However, though she knew God forgave her, she was unsure of how Rich would feel. She loved him greatly, but was afraid to risk losing him. There were a few times during the courtship when she almost brought up the topic, but she would always back down. Feeling that he wouldn't understand the circumstances and afraid that he would leave her, she didn't tell Rich about her past.

Six months after the wedding, the two were testifying in a civil court on behalf of Operation Rescue. The prosecutor asked Abby questions concerning empathy she might feel toward the women going into abortion clinics. She picked up a hesitation in Abby's voice and out of nowhere asked if Abby had ever had an abortion. Abby was caught off guard. She was reminded she was under oath. She broke down in tears and answered with the truth.

Rich was stunned and horrified. As Abby sobbed and related her past, he ran out of the courtroom. Common life between the two ended that day in the courtroom. Rich moved out of their home and chose never to speak to Abby again. Rich left and lost everything that day—a woman he had loved, a woman who still loved him and a potential life of happiness.

This case is obviously troublesome, as it deals with the pro-life cause vis-à-vis abortion, the issue of life versus death. As uncomfortable as the circumstances of the case are, the marriage may be declared null on the ground of imposed error. Rich invalidly contracted marriage on the wedding day because he had been deceived by Abby regarding her past. She had withheld information about the abortion for fear Rich would not marry her. As his later behavior proved, she was correct in her assumption. He would never have married her had he known about the abortion. Though a wedding had occurred, no marriage came about that day.

Q. 38. What does it mean to be in error concerning the unity, indissolubility or sacramental dignity of marriage?

One is **ready** for marriage if one has requisite knowledge. A person must know that the Church teaches that marriage is exclusive, permanent and a sacrament.[92] This is the teaching of the Church regarding marriage. Yet, some people hold beliefs about marriage that are contrary to the Church's teaching. Now the simple fact that a person may believe marriage to be something other than that which the Church teaches doesn't in itself render consent invalid, as long as the individual marries according to the Church's mindset. However, if an individual knows what the Church teaches, but marries according to his or her own mindset, then that person marries invalidly. A wedding may take place, but a valid marriage does not.

This ground concerning error focuses on a person's intellect and will. Since these concepts are complex and subtle, sweeping generalizations cannot be made; for example, it cannot be said that every atheist marrying a Catholic does so invalidly due to error regarding the sacramentality of marriage. An atheist may not believe marriage to be a sacrament, but may know and accept the fact that the Church considers this to be so. So each case must be examined on its merits to determine whether or not a person's erroneous ideas affected his or her intentions on the wedding day.

This particular ground is often used in cases regarding the consent of people who hold beliefs that are alien or hostile to those of the Catholic Church. It may also affect the consent of baptized nonbelievers, that is, individuals who have been baptized Catholic, but do not in any way practice or hold to the tenets of their faith. Proof for this ground of nullity must rest on the fact that the error was present on the wedding day and that it determined the person's will—no easy task!

A CASE: Hope, a Roman Catholic, married Lenny. He had been baptized a Methodist as a child, but became an agnostic communist in his late teens. They truly loved one another and had much in common. They also held different worldviews on some matters. They enjoyed having long, intellectual talks on many subjects, especially religion and politics. Though Lenny respected Hope's religious convictions, he made it clear that he was opposed to organized religion and many of its principles.

Despite these differences, the couple married. Hope "intended" a lifelong commitment and Lenny "hoped" the commitment would last for life. Unfortunately, after three years of marriage and one child, the marriage was over. One day Lenny simply walked out. He was unhappy with the responsibilities of marriage and family. It was much more than he had expected. Hope was devastated.

Four years later Hope petitioned the Church for a declaration of nullity based on the ground of Lenny's error concerning marriage. The facts of the case indicated that Lenny knew that the Church holds marriage to be indissoluble, a lifelong commitment that no power can dissolve. In fact, the couple had attended Pre-Cana classes prior to the wedding where this was discussed. The priest preparing them had taken extra care to discuss the nature of marriage with Lenny, because he realized it was important for Lenny to understand the nature of the marriage covenant.

However, neither Hope nor the priest knew the degree to which Lenny held an opposite view. He did not accept the Church's teaching regarding indissolubility; he believed marriage was quite dissoluble. Sadly, he had witnessed many unhappy marriages of relatives and friends. As he had told Hope during the courtship, despite the tenets of the Catholic Church, he was convinced that any unhappy marriage should be dissolved by divorce. In fact, he had encouraged friends to divorce when he saw them in unhappy marriages. The depth of his belief system regarding marriage was verified when he walked out on his wife and son because he was "unhappy." The tribunal investigation clarified that despite the Church's position regarding indissolubility, Lenny elected to enter his marriage to Hope based on what he understood marriage to be—a contract that can be dissolved. There certainly had been a wedding, but the marriage was invalid from its beginning.

Q. 39. What does it mean to "simulate" marriage?

When persons marry they **will** to bring about the sacred bond of marriage, whether they enter into a Christian marriage or a good and natural marriage. If any of the essential "elements" or "properties" of marriage, or marriage itself, are excluded on the day of the wedding, the consent of the party(ies) is defective and the marriage is invalid.[93] The word exclusion is synonymous with simulation. The legal presumption on the wedding day is that the person wills what he or she says. Common sense dictates that the person means the vows they publicly exchange.[94]

When a person simulates marriage, he or she is basically lying. The wedding vows intend one meaning, but the person intends another. Proof of simulation is often summed up by the maxim *actions speak louder than words*. Though a person may say "I do" on the wedding day, if all of the subsequent actions of the person say "I don't," then it is clear that the person simulated consent. The vows are rendered meaningless, and so the marriage is declared null. There was a wedding, but the marriage was invalid from its beginning.

Total simulation is the act of externally feigning consent and internally excluding marriage. In other words a person may go through a wedding ceremony for a reason extraneous to marriage. This individual had no desire to establish the partnership of life with the other person. The end result is an arrangement that is a fake, an imitation of marriage. The reason behind this fakery is called the "motive" for simulation.

Marriage, or the right to the partnership of life, can be totally excluded from consent in three ways. First, if the parties exclude cohabitation, they have no intention of living together as husband and wife. For instance, a man and a woman marry simply to fulfill a legal requirement. Joe marries Imelda so that she may obtain a "green card" for immigration purposes. They never live together after the ceremony. Though they may have had a wedding ceremony, the marriage was invalid from its beginning.

Second, persons may go through a wedding ceremony simply for an extraneous reason. In this instance the ceremony becomes a means to an end. For example, suppose a man is in jail for rape and he learns that he can gain early release if he marries. He goes through the ceremony simply as a means of getting out of prison. After his release he never sees the woman again. Though they may have had a wedding ceremony, the marriage was invalid from its beginning.

Finally, there is a total exclusion of marriage when a person substitutes his or her own ideas of marriage for true marriage. For example, a man may consider marriage to be simply a contractual arrangement. He basically "hires" a beautiful woman to be a social companion and hostess, a trophy wife and nothing more. He treats her as an employee during common life and never establishes the partnership of the whole of life—a partnership that the Church calls marriage. Though they may have had a wedding ceremony, there is no marriage.

Partial simulation is the exclusion of an essential "element" or "property" of marriage. The elements, or parts, of marriage are the "good of the spouses" and the procreation and education of children.[95] The essential properties, or characteristics, of marriage are unity and indissolubility.[96] In addition, sacramental dignity pertains to the essence of Christian marriage.[97] Most legal experts hold sacramentality to be either an element or property of marriage, though some suggest it is both.

A visual representation for the concept of partial simulation is a pie. Think of a whole pie as the covenant of marriage. The pieces of the pie are the essential elements and properties of marriage; as such, these individual pieces constitute the whole. However, if one of the pieces is removed, the whole no longer exists.

Suppose you purchased a whole pie from the bakery window and returned home to find a piece missing; you did not receive what you agreed to purchase. The baker withheld a piece of pie and the sale was dishonest. You were cheated. This is what happens with partial simulation in marriage.

If a person partially simulates on the wedding day, he or she wants to be married, but denies the other person the right to a particular dimension of marriage. For instance, a man may want to marry because he wants a wife with whom he can spend the rest of his life. However, if he has no intention of ever having children, then his consent is invalid due to partial simulation—he excluded the "good of children." A woman may want to marry because she has always wanted children and a permanent commitment. Yet, if she has also decided to continue her affair with her old boyfriend, then her consent is defective due to partial simulation—the exclusion of fidelity. Their intended spouses have been cheated out of an essential property of marriage. They have been lied to by the one simulating consent.

Q. 40. How is an intention against children manifested?

When persons marry, they **will** to bring about the sacred bond of marriage, whether they enter into a Christian marriage or a good and natural marriage. The legal presumption on the wedding day is that the person actually wills what he or she says. Common sense dictates that persons mean the vows they publicly exchange.[98] However, if a person excludes an essential element or property of marriage on the day of the wedding, then that person's consent is defective and the marriage is invalid.[99]

This question focuses on an intention against an essential element of marriage, namely, children.[100] However, the phrase "an intention against children" is somewhat misleading. The intention is not an exclusion of children, since children are a gift from God and no one has a "right" to this gift. Rather, the exclusion of this ground is a denial of the right to sexual intercourse, that is, to noncontraceptive intercourse—intercourse that is open to conception. It is in this sense that the phrase an "intention against children" is to be interpreted. This clarification is crucial, for it impacts upon the consent of persons who are sterile on the wedding day. Sterility does not invalidate marriage, since the right that is being exchanged is the right to sexual intercourse. A sterile person is quite capable of exchanging that right.

If procreative intercourse is always impeded by contraceptives, then children will not be conceived. By refusing to exchange the right of procreative intercourse, the possibility of children is thereby denied in the marriage. A couple that decides before marriage that they will never give each other the right to have children marries invalidly. They have stood up publicly and said "I do" on the wedding day to all that marriage entails, including the good of children. Yet, if all of their subsequent actions say "I don't" in regard to conception, then the marriage could subsequently be declared invalid due to an intention against children.

The openness to procreation and life is also implied in the "right to noncontraceptive intercourse." Thus, a woman who performs the marital act in a natural way, but then always uses spermicides or pessaries, or takes a "morning after" pill, or practices abortion or infanticide has excluded children. She has married invalidly.

One cannot deny that Western cultures are infused with a "contraceptive mentality." This cultural phenomenon may impact upon a couple's consent. If a couple enters into an agreement before marriage to postpone children for a few years through the use of artificial contraceptives (questions of morality notwithstanding), this does not necessarily mean that children have been excluded. They may have exchanged the right to children, but are simply postponing the exercise of that right. However, the opposite is also true if the agreement of postponement becomes more important than the whole covenant of marriage.

A CASE: Noah and Kitty decided not to have children right away. Noah was raised in a large family and really wanted children; Kitty was more ambivalent. Nonetheless, they had agreed before marriage to postpone a family for five to seven years. Kitty was beginning medical school and Noah was starting a new job, so finances justified the delay. From the outset of the marriage, they practiced artificial birth control; he used a condom and she used an IUD.

Within two years Noah had soared ahead in his career. They had a home, a car and financial security. Though Kitty was still struggling with school, finances were no longer an issue. Noah decided it was time to start a family. He told Kitty he wanted to have a child. Kitty couldn't believe he was backing out of their agreed-upon postponement. She was horrified that he wanted her to continue school and have a child. They argued over the matter for six months, but she refused to change her mind. On one occasion Kitty realized Noah had had intercourse without a condom. She felt betrayed and refused intercourse from that moment onward. Just before their third wedding anniversary, they divorced.

Noah petitioned the Church for a declaration of nullity based on Kitty's intention against the good of children.

Both Noah and Kitty gave testimony to the court. It was apparent from their testimony and the testimony of witnesses that her intention not to have children was firm, intense, inflexible and nonnegotiable. The agreement of postponement was not subordinate to the marriage covenant. Rather, for Kitty, this agreement superseded the marriage covenant and its inherent right to noncontraceptive intercourse.

Noah had the right to request noncontraceptive intercourse; Kitty denied him this right. His request was legitimate, but she had not bargained for the fact that he might change his mind regarding the delay. There was no way she would allow conception during medical school, regardless of finances or any other fact. In essence, it was clear to the court that she had excluded the right to noncontraceptive sexual intercourse and thus had entered marriage invalidly. Kitty excluded children and thus cheated Noah out of an essential element of marriage. There certainly had been a wedding, but the marriage was invalid from its beginning.

Q. 41. What is an intention against fidelity?

When persons marry they **will** to bring about the sacred bond of marriage, whether they enter into a Christian marriage or a good and natural marriage. The legal presumption on the wedding day is that the person wills what he or she says. Common sense dictates that persons mean the vows they publicly exchange.[101] However, if a person excludes an essential element or property of marriage on the day of the wedding, then that person's consent is defective and the marriage is invalid.[102]

This question focuses on an intention against a property of marriage, namely, fidelity.[103] Thus, both polygamy and adultery are excluded. A person has the right to be the one and only spouse—neither party has the right to be polygamous. One also has the right to sexual fidelity, that is, having one's spouse as one's only sex partner. This excludes a partner's right to engage in sexual relations with any person, whether of the opposite or the same sex.

It is important to note that the exclusion of fidelity must be present on the wedding day for a marriage to be invalid for this reason. Certainly, if a woman marries and intends to keep up an ongoing relationship with her lover, she has excluded fidelity and married invalidly. But suppose a man marries intending to be faithful to his wife for life and twelve years into the marriage he has an affair. That is a sin, not an intention against fidelity. As with many cases of partial simulation, situations are not always that black and white; there are areas of gray in regard to consent.

A CASE: Hugh began dating Chastity when he was age thirty and she was age twenty-seven. Hugh had been a playboy all of his adult life. In fact, the couple had been sexually active during their two-year courtship. Chastity knew his history, and they had had discussions concerning marital fidelity. However, now that he had found Chastity, Hugh wanted to settle down and marry.

Hugh really hoped he would remain faithful. Nevertheless, he confided to his best man that given human weakness, this was not a very realistic hope or expectation for him. Though he knew that Chastity and the Church believed fidelity was possible, Hugh had his doubts.

They married, then subsequently divorced after five years of marriage and two children. The divorce was brought on due to Hugh's constant infidelities. Chastity petitioned the Church for a declaration of nullity based on Hugh's partial simulation: his exclusion of fidelity. The proceedings uncovered the fact that Hugh grew up witnessing his father's multiple infidelities against his mother. This was the role modeling he received in childhood concerning a husband/wife relationship. The best man testified that Hugh never believed fidelity was possible. In addition this witness swore that three weeks after the honeymoon, Hugh was having sex outside of marriage. It became clear to the court that even though Hugh stood up on the day of the wedding and said "I do," all of his subsequent actions in regard to fidelity said "I don't." He excluded fidelity, and thus cheated Chastity out of an essential property of marriage. There certainly had been a wedding, but the marriage was invalid from its beginning.

Q. 42. What is an intention against perpetuity?

When persons marry, they **will** to bring about the sacred bond of marriage, whether they enter into a Christian marriage or a good and natural marriage. The legal presumption on the wedding day is that the person wills what he or she says. Common sense dictates that the persons mean the vows they publicly exchange.[104] However, if a person excludes an essential element or property of marriage on the day of the wedding, then that person's consent is defective and the marriage is invalid.[105]

This question focuses on an intention against a property of marriage, namely, perpetuity, a lifelong commitment.[106] Perpetuity refers to indissolubility, and this is a property of all marriages. Perpetuity is more than permanence. Something is permanent only for as long as it lasts. Whereas something is perpetual when it is everlasting. Permanence admits to degrees, but perpetuity does not.

Marriage is a lifelong commitment that cannot be dissolved; rather, it is indissoluble. If a person consents to a marital union that is something less than indissoluble, then that person does not bring about a marriage, as the Church understands marriage. This ground is often evidenced in cultures that have a pervasive divorce mentality. It could also be applicable if a person espouses the tenets of a religion that does not support the indissolubility of marriage as part of its beliefs.

A CASE: Elizabeth, a baptized nonpracticing Christian,

married Peter, a baptized Roman Catholic. Both were thirty years of age and had dated for five years. Elizabeth is a child of divorce. Her parents divorced after many unhappy years together, primarily due to her father's drinking. Elizabeth was twelve at that time.

Elizabeth's father went on with his life after the divorce simply playing the field and moving from one relationship to the next. Her mother remarried within a year. However, her mother divorced this second husband four years later (he turned out to be an abusive alcoholic). At the time of the wedding, Elizabeth's mother was just living with a man and appeared happy.

Elizabeth's childhood left her longing for a stable relationship. After being in numerous relationships but never happy, she finally found Peter. She was truly in love with him. She was happy and fulfilled in the relationship and "hoped" that their marriage would last forever. She had seen people who were unhappy, both alone and together. She wanted her life to be different. Elizabeth entered the marriage with the mindset, "I plan to be married for life—as long as I am happy."

Six years into the marriage and two children later, Peter began to drink to excess. After a year of failed attempts at Alcoholics Anonymous and one detoxification admission, Elizabeth had had enough and left the marital home. She found herself in the same situation she had endured as a child—alcohol and abuse. There was no way she was going to stay in a marriage that involved this type of deprivation. Though the reality of what lay ahead saddened her, she believed in the solution of divorce. She had survived it and so would her children. She left Peter, took the children and moved on with her life in search of happiness elsewhere.

Peter petitioned the court for a declaration of nullity based on Elizabeth's intention against perpetuity. Though he had overcome the signs of his addiction, Elizabeth had no intentions of returning to the marriage. In fact, she had remarried a year after the divorce became final. He claimed her vows of "in good times and in bad" and "till death do us part" were meaningless. Though she had said, "I do," her subsequent action of divorce said, "I don't."

Peter presented witnesses to the court who testified to Elizabeth's firmly held belief in divorce. She had advised them to divorce when their marriages had become unhappy. Her brother testified that though Elizabeth had hoped her marriage to Peter would be forever, she also believed that divorce was an acceptable option. In the end the marriage was declared null on the ground of Elizabeth's partial simulation—an intention against a lifelong commitment. She excluded perpetuity, and thus cheated Peter out of an essential property of marriage. There certainly had been a wedding, but the marriage was invalid from its beginning.

Q. 43. How is an intention against the "good of the spouses" manifested?

When persons marry they **will** to bring about the sacred bond of marriage, whether they enter into a Christian marriage or a good and natural marriage. The legal presumption on the wedding day is that the person wills what he or she says. Common sense dictates that the person means the vows that are publicly exchanged.[107] However, if a person excludes an essential element or property of marriage on the day of the wedding, then that person's consent is defective and the marriage is invalid.[108]

This question focuses on an intention against an essential element of marriage, namely, the good of the spouses.[109] When two persons enter into marriage, they form a marital covenant. They enter into a partnership of the whole of life that involves "the good of the spouses." The law does not determine what constitutes the good of the spouses. However, it is reasonable to conclude that the party(ies) must not exclude the interpersonal relationship of husband and wife.

It happens that individuals marry intending to use or abuse their spouses. They decide beforehand that they will not be loving or caring, but simply abuse their spouse for their own selfish reasons. These persons marry invalidly.

A CASE: Jerry dated Violet for two years before they were married. He was a perfect gentleman. Unfortunately, his family was unable to attend the wedding. In fact, Violet had never met his family, as they lived out of state. Nor had Jerry spoken much about his childhood. These facts never meant much to Violet, but in hindsight they proved to be ominous signposts.

What Violet didn't know was that Jerry had had a horrific childhood. He had witnessed his father constantly beat his mother. This was his modeling of a husband/wife relationship. Jerry actually resented his mother more than his father because she had stayed in the abusive relationship. Both he and his sister had suffered greatly at his father's hands, and he despised his mother for her constant excuses. Jerry hated his parents and was filled with unresolved rage. However, he had learned to control this rage very well—that is, until he married.

The nightmare for Violet began on the honeymoon. They did not make love that first night; rather, he raped her. Her cries of pain meant nothing to him. The next day the verbal insults started. He constantly degraded her and mocked her tone of voice when she tried to stand up to him. Violet was in shock. The more she tried to appease Jerry, the more abusive in behavior he became; this behavior continued after the honeymoon. Fortunately, Violet did not repeat the same mistake that Jerry's mother had made. She had the good sense to leave Jerry one month after the wedding. She knew instinctively that abuse has no place in the community of life and love that is marriage.

Violet petitioned the Church for a declaration of nul-

lity based on Jerry's intention against the good of the
spouses. Witnesses verified Jerry's abusive behavior. His
sister testified to the abuse they had endured as children.
It was clear to the court that though Jerry stood up publicly and said, "I do" on the wedding day, all of his subsequent actions said "I don't." He excluded the good of the
spouses, and thus cheated Violet out of an essential element of marriage. There certainly had been a wedding,
but the marriage was invalid from its beginning.

Q. 44. What is an intention against the sacramentality of marriage?

When persons marry, they **will** to bring about the sacred
bond of marriage, whether they enter into a Christian marriage or a good and natural marriage. The legal presumption on the wedding day is that the person wills what he or
she says. Common sense dictates that the person means the
vows that are publicly exchanged.[110] However, if a person
excludes an essential element or property of marriage on
the day of the wedding, then that person's consent is defective and the marriage is invalid.[111]

This question focuses on an intention against the sacramental nature of marriage.[112] It is concerned only with
Christian marriages, since they are sacramental. It is not
concerned with good and natural marriages, which are
nonsacramental. Keep in mind that in the Latin Church the
ministers of a sacramental marriage are a baptized bride
and groom. This particular ground admits to one of two
possibilities. First, it can happen that a baptized Catholic
has fallen away from the faith. If such a person has a true
animosity toward the Church, he or she may consider the
Church's teaching on sacraments to be superstition, and as
such, may reject the idea that marriage is a sacrament. This
person may have a church wedding only to please his or her
parents, but in no way believe in marriage's sacramentality.

The second instance would involve a baptized Protestant who marries in accord with the teaching of his or her church. That particular church's teaching may reject the notion of marriage as a sacrament. In this instance, as with the one above, it's hard to admit that a person administers or receives a sacrament when he or she does not believe marriage is a sacrament. Yet the teaching of the Catholic Church is clear: when the baptized marry, they must intend to do what the Church does; they intend to bring about a sacramental union.

A CASE: Faith, a devout Catholic, had dated Thomas, a lapsed Catholic who had become an atheist, for about three years before they married. They were aware of their differences regarding religion and faith. He never minded that she went to church during their courtship, but he expected her to respect his decision to have nothing to do with organized religion. Basically, Thomas doubted everything the Church proposed as truth.

Thomas' rejection of the faith was so pronounced that after the engagement he made it clear he did not want a church wedding. He thought that the Church's rituals were simply superstitious and silly. Faith prevailed upon him to go through with the church ceremony. It was important to her and her parents, as well as his parents. He acquiesced to her wishes, but under protest. He agreed to the church wedding, as long as she understood that he was only doing this for her.

After the wedding the couple began their life together as husband and wife. They had three children during their eight years of marriage. However, the marriage was difficult from its outset. They constantly argued, often about religion. During the courtship, Thomas had respected Faith's wishes to attend church. After the wedding however, he began to mock her. He constantly put her down because of her religious practices. When the children were born, there was a battle over their baptisms. In fact, Thomas did not attend any of the baptisms and was always out of the house for the celebrations afterward. He thought that the whole idea of forcing children into a religion at infancy was ludicrous.

The argument that surrounded their ultimate separation was over their eldest son's First Communion. Thomas ranted at his wife and son over their religious superstitions. He refused to attend the ceremony or allow a party back at the house afterward. In fact, the marital relationship had become so dysfunctional that he flew into a rage and ripped their son's First Communion jacket in two. Faith told him to leave, and he never returned.

After the divorce Faith petitioned the Church for a declaration of nullity on the grounds of Thomas's partial simulation on the day of the wedding, namely, his intention against the sacramentality of marriage. Surprisingly, Thomas participated in the tribunal investigation, but in opposition. His participation in the tribunal process became an opportunity for him to state publicly to the institutional Church that he believed its faith to be meaningless. He testified that he married in the Church only to please Faith and their parents. He corroborated all that Faith and the witnesses had said regarding his antipathy to the Church.

Thomas's opposition to a declaration of nullity was based on the fact that he believed his marriage to be a valid union, albeit nonsacramental. Yet, this opposition was the summation of proof in regard to the grounds of the case. Thomas never intended his marriage to be a sacrament; to him, it was simply a civil contract. However, a marriage between two baptized individuals is by its very nature sacramental. Thomas's rejection of this reality was indeed partial simulation. He excluded sacramentality and thus cheated Faith out of an essential property and element of marriage. There certainly had been a wedding, but the marriage was invalid from its beginning.

Q. 45. How would a condition placed on consent render a marriage invalid?

When persons marry, they **will** to bring about the sacred bond of marriage, whether they enter into a Christian marriage or a good and natural marriage. The legal presumption on the wedding day is that the person wills what he or she says. Common sense dictates that the person means the vows that are publicly exchanged.[113] No conditions may be placed on the consent of the party(ies). If future conditions are placed on the wedding day, the marriage is invalid.[114] If conditions are placed regarding the past or present, they may or may not invalidate the marriage, depending on the circumstances.[115]

Prior to November 27, 1983 (the effective date of the 1983 Code of Canon Law) a future condition placed on a marriage only invalidated consent if the condition went unfulfilled. For example, Connie and Burt marry in 1970. Connie marries on the condition that Burt will soon inherit a substantial sum of money. If the money is inherited within the first few years of marriage, the marriage is valid. If he does not inherit the money, the marriage is invalid.

However, a future condition placed on a marriage after the 1983 Code of Canon Law went into effect would immediately invalidate consent. If Connie married Burt in 1990 under the same condition mentioned above, then the marriage is invalid from the wedding day, regardless of any inheritance.

When the condition is more important than marriage itself, then the condition invalidates the marriage. It is important to note that the person placing the condition does not have to be aware of its invalidating effect. It is enough that the party ranks the condition of higher importance than the marriage. It is enough for the individual to hold that without the circumstance or the quality present in the condition, he or she would not want the marriage. The condition must have an objective importance and affect the future life of the couple—for example, the absence of a sexually transmitted disease or sexual perversion. Thus, the conditioning of a marriage may be explicit or very subtle, but it must be a true condition of particular importance.

A CASE: Barbie was an all-American girl. She was captain of her high school and college cheerleading teams. She had won numerous beauty pageant awards throughout her teens and early twenties. No one was surprised when she started dating Butch in college. He was bright, handsome and the captain of both the football and baseball teams. They made the ideal couple.

Barbie's goal in life was to be the consummate wife and mother. She idolized her parents' marriage. Her father was a successful businessman and her mother was devoted to husband, children and home. Barbie adored Butch, and he adored her. He didn't treat her as an object, but as a person. Furthermore, he had always been a gentleman throughout the courtship; though they had engaged in some heavy petting, they respected boundaries and avoided premarital sex. She couldn't wait to be married; to love and be loved by Butch for the rest of her life.

Though they had a picture-perfect courtship and wedding, the marriage ended in civil divorce in less than a year. Barbie petitioned the Church for a declaration of nullity on the ground of a future condition. As she told the judge, she had always wanted a husband who was masculine and loving.

She had spent close to forty minutes in the bathroom getting ready for bed on the wedding night. All of her beauty training had paid off. As she looked in the mirror, she realized that she was drop-dead gorgeous. She had on the most beautiful negligee in the world. However, when she opened the door she discovered that Butch had on a negligee as well!

To her horror, Butch announced he needed to wear women's undergarments to become sexually aroused for intercourse. All of her dreams concerning a strong, masculine husband were shattered that first night. She never recovered emotionally from the shock of seeing her husband dressed as a woman.

She actually stayed in the marriage for about ten months. It took that long for her to leave because no one would understand what went wrong. She loved Butch and didn't want to ruin his reputation. At the same time, she never once made love to him under those circumstances, even that first night; she could not. She intended to marry a masculine man, one who treated her like a woman, not the other way around.

During the tribunal investigation Butch and Barbie both testified to the same facts. Barbie presented witnesses who elaborated on her desire to model a traditional husband/wife relationship; this was without a doubt a condition placed on her intention for marriage. It was clear to the court that she married Butch believing him to be the perfect role model of a man. If she had known the truth to the contrary, she never would have married him. There certainly had been a wedding, but the marriage was invalid from its beginning.

Q. 46. What does it mean when a marriage is declared null on force and fear?

When persons marry they **will** to bring about the sacred bond of marriage, whether they enter into a Christian marriage or a good and natural marriage. The legal presumption on the wedding day is that the person wills what he or she says. Common sense dictates that the person means the vows that are publicly exchanged.[116] The act of consent must be free. If it is forced or there is an excessive amount of fear brought to bear on the person's consent, then the marriage was invalid from its beginning.[117]

Force refers to an external physical or moral impulse that cannot be resisted. It is a coercion of the person's will. In a forced marriage a person is unable to choose his or her spouse. Consent issued under force is always invalid. An easy example is a shotgun wedding. An agent holds a gun to a person and makes him or her say, "I do." The vow is meaningless. There may be a wedding, but there is no valid marriage.

Fear is intimidation. It results from an impending danger or evil. Consent issued under fear may be invalid if the conditions set down in law are met. The fear must be grave, extrinsic to the person and the cause of the wedding. First, the fear must be grave—for example, threats of death, imprisonment or disinheritance. Second, the fear must be extrinsic to the person, that is, it must be imposed from outside the person. It cannot simply result from a suggestion or suspicion in the person's mind. Third, the grave fear must also be the cause of the marriage. A person marries in order to free himself or herself from the fear. Put simply, the marriage in question is invalid if it was contracted **because** of fear. However, the issues are not always black and white, but oftentimes gray.

There are two types of fear distinguished in law: common fear and reverential fear. Common fear is derived from threats made by a hostile person. Reverential fear arises out of an expectation of harm by causing displeasure to someone to whom special reverence is owed, such as a parent, guardian or superior.

A CASE: Sarah was shy as both a child and a teenager. Though she grew up in Brooklyn, New York, she had a very sheltered home life. Her family was ethnic in an old-world European sense. It was also very extended; she had dozens of aunts, uncles and cousins. Her mother stayed home and raised the children while her father ran the house with an iron fist. She viewed her life as happy and fulfilled.

However, there was a frightening memory she lived with daily. Her older sister, Ruth, had become pregnant out of wedlock. When her father found out, he erupted with rage. He threw her out of the house, destroyed all of her clothes, disinherited her and she was never spoken of again. She was "dead" to the family because of the dishonor she had brought upon them. This event was seared into the memories of the other six children, Sarah being the next girl in line.

One can only imagine Sarah's shock and fear when she realized she was pregnant. She had dated Danny her senior year of high school and her first year in the work force. However they broke up a month before she discovered she was pregnant because she desired to date others. She knew he wasn't the man she wanted to be with for the rest of her life. But now she was pregnant and everything changed. She confided in her brother. He told her what she already knew. Their father's reaction would be immediate and swift; she too would be disowned. She had no choice; she had to marry and do so quickly.

Danny had truly loved Sarah, so he was not difficult to convince. Sarah then talked her parents into a small and hasty wedding. She convinced them of the depth of her love for Danny and lied to them, saying that he was being transferred immediately to another state for work. Though she hated lying, she knew she had to do so in order to marry. Unlike Ruth, she was petrified of losing her family. Marriage was the only way out of the predicament, and it worked.

The marriage was over in three years. Danny quickly realized that he had been used by Sarah. In retaliation he began an affair with a coworker and left Sarah and their child. Sarah petitioned the Church for a declaration of nullity based on the ground of reverential fear. The facts of the case were corroborated by the parties and witnesses. It was clear to the court that Sarah's consent was defective because it was not free. There certainly had been a wedding, but the marriage was invalid from its beginning.

Q. 47. What is defective convalidation?

A marriage may be invalid on the wedding day due to: the existence of an impediment that renders the ministers unqualified to give consent, a defect of their consent or a defect of the form required for marriage.[118] If the parties are happily married and realize that any one of these defects existed on the wedding day, they may choose to convalidate the marriage. In other words, they choose to make their invalid marriage valid. The law specifies how this is to be done in each situation.[119]

If the original consent of either or both of the parties needs to be convalidated because a diriment impediment existed on the wedding day, the impediment must first cease to exist. Then, the party or parties who were aware of its existence must acknowledge the invalidity of their union and make a new act of consent.[120] If convalidation is required because there was a defect of consent on the wedding day, then the party whose consent was defective must acknowledge the invalidity and give new consent.[121] If convalidation is required because of a defect of form on the wedding day, both parties must acknowledge invalidity and place new consent to bring about a valid marriage. If the new consent is not properly given, this could amount to total simulation.

As complicated as that is, it can happen that after the convalidation the couple is no longer happy. Given these circumstances, suppose that they then divorce, and one of the parties later petitions the Church for a declaration of nullity based on **defective convalidation!** This petition suggests that one or both of the parties did not give proper consent when they convalidated their marriage. It must be proven that the legal specifications had not been fulfilled; if so, the convalidation is declared invalid.

A declaration of this sort declares invalid the convalidation of an invalid marriage! This concept is so dense that it's like legal quicksand.

A CASE: Caroline, a Catholic, had married Peter, a Protestant, in the Catholic Church in 1970. Her uncle, Father Mark, witnessed the exchange of consent. Three years later, the couple discovered that Father Mark had never received the necessary delegation to perform the ceremony. So, in effect, their marriage was invalid in church law due to a defect of form! Caroline was horrified, but Peter was amused and thought the whole matter was no big deal. In fact he remembered Father Mark saying something in the sacristy before the wedding about forgetting to contact the bishop, but the two just laughed it off. Father Mark couldn't be bothered "jumping through hoops."

Nonetheless, Caroline persuaded Peter to go through another wedding ceremony. They drove down to the rectory and exchanged their vows in front of the parish priest and two witnesses. Caroline was very relieved; now they were married in the eyes of the Church.

Unfortunately, the couple divorced five years after this convalidation. Caroline then petitioned the Church for a declaration of nullity based on Peter's defective convalidation. Upon reflection, she believed that Peter did not place a new act of consent at the time of convalidation. Fortunately, Peter also testified. At first he was quite hostile to the tribunal because their forms implied that the couple had been married for only five years. He corrected the court and stated they had been married for eight years. He argued that their marriage came about when he and Caroline stood in front of Father Mark and their families. He told the court that he believed the rectory ceremony was unnecessary. It was simply something they had to do; it was some foolish matter of Church "legalese."

It was apparent to the court that Peter did not acknowledge the first wedding ceremony as invalid, nor did he place a new act of consent when they went to the rectory. The tribunal declared that the validation was invalid due to his lack of consent.

In this case, there had been a church wedding ceremony, but the marriage was invalid due to a defect of form. This was followed by a second wedding ceremony, but that marriage was also invalid due to a defect of consent, namely, defective convalidation.

PART IV:

The Church As Witness

The law states that marriage is brought about through: (1) the consent of the bride and groom, (2) legitimately manifested, (3) by those qualified according to the law (again, the bride and the groom).[122] *Thus, if it is determined that the consent of the parties was not legitimately manifested, then marriage was* NOT *brought about.*[123] *This section moves away from the consent of the parties. The ministers' consent is not called into question; rather the authority of the Church official who witnessed the exchange of consent is questioned, or the required number of witnesses was insufficient.*

Marriage is both a private and a public act; it has many social consequences since it impacts upon the welfare of the community. Therefore, the act of marrying is public and regulated by law. This is an easy concept to grasp because it is true not only in the Church, but also in the State. For example, the State may require blood tests, a marriage license and a duly appointed official, as well as witnesses, to observe the couple's exchange of consent. The Church demands similar, though not identical requirements.

This section will explore the regulations of the Church

and the legal implications that result when these require-
ments are not fulfilled. If the official lacked the authority to
witness the couple's exchange of vows, or the requisite wit-
nesses were not present, then the marriage can be declared
null by reason of a defect of form. In other words, if the
proper form surrounding the marriage ceremony had not
been observed, then a valid marriage was NOT brought about
on the wedding day.

Q. 48. What is the proper "form of marriage"?

The **form of marriage** requires the presence of an official witness who assists the parties at the time of consent, as well as two witnesses who are present for the exchange of vows. Whenever a Catholic marries, this form is required, unless dispensed from, for the marriage to be valid.[124]

The external control over a couple's exchange of consent was introduced into the Church at the Council of Trent (1545–63).[125] The laws issued to govern this exchange came about in response to an abuse that had developed in various countries. Up until that time marriage could be a private celebration between the parties alone, since consent alone made marriage. However, this led to clandestine (secret) marriages, which presented many pastoral problems for the Church.

Suppose Guinevere fell in love with Lancelot and the two ran off to a glade and exchanged consent. They were married, since consent makes marriage, but only they knew it. If, three months later, Guinevere fell in love with Rupert and ran off to the river and exchanged consent, Rupert considered her his wife; but this was not true—a fact known only to Guinevere.

Now suppose Lancelot and Rupert discovered that both

had secretly exchanged consent with Guinevere. They publicly accuse her of the deceit, but she denies it. No one could be certain of the truth because no one witnessed either exchange of consent. Both unions had been clandestine marriages. So, legally, Guinevere would be free to marry Arthur in the village church, if she so desired, since no one had witnessed the previous exchanges of vows!

The problem was a real one, and the legislation from the Council of Trent attempted to address this pastoral issue. The council decreed that persons had to marry in the presence of their parish priest (or another priest delegated to take his place), as well as two or three witnesses. These requirements would address the difficulties brought on by clandestine marriages and also reinforce the public dimensions of marriage. If a couple exchanged their consent without fulfilling these specifications, their marriage was invalid in the Church. It had no public effects in law and the parties were not bound to it.

For numerous historical reasons, Trent's decree regarding the form of marriage was not well implemented. It wasn't until the early twentieth century (1908) that all Catholics, everywhere, were bound to follow this canonical form when they married. If they did not, there was no marriage in the eyes of the Church.

Unfortunately, the universal application of this law led to an imbalance between the public and private dimensions of marriage. Attention to the proper form began to take precedence over the substance of marriage. The legal requirements the Church placed upon the exchange of consent became more important than consent itself. It was not until the 1983 Code of Canon Law that a more balanced approach was formulated. The proper form is still crucial due to the public dimensions of marriage, but the substance of marriage, consent, allows exceptions to the form. A Catholic can be dispensed from the form of marriage if he or she marries a non-Catholic person, Christian or not.

In addition, delegation for the priest or deacon has been made easier. Finally, if there is a technical fault present in the form, the Church will supply what was missing.[126]

Q. 49. Who is the proper official of marriage?

The *Catechism of the Catholic Church* states:

> The priest (or deacon) who assists at the celebration of a marriage receives the consent of the spouses in the name of the Church and gives the blessings of the Church. The presence of the Church's minister (and also the witnesses) visibly expresses the fact that marriage is an ecclesial reality.[127]

This excerpt from the *Catechism* is supported by the law's specification regarding the officiant of marriage. This person is deputed by the Church to request that the parties declare their consent and to receive their consent in the name of the Church.[128] It is clear that the proper official actively "assists" at the wedding. The official is normally a priest or deacon; but when there is a lack of priests or deacons in a certain place, the bishop can delegate lay persons to assist at marriages according to the provisions set down in law. For example, a diocese may have very few priests and be quite large territorially. In order to facilitate the Church celebration of marriages, the bishop may name a layman or laywoman as the proper official.[129]

Q. 50. Who is bound to the form of marriage?

Only Catholics are bound to the form of marriage. The law stipulates that a baptized Catholic who has not left the Church by a formal act must exchange consent in the presence of the proper official of marriage (unless this requirement is dispensed). In most cases this means that a Catholic is to marry in the presence of a duly appointed priest or deacon. The presence of this official is required for validity.[130]

So, for example, if two Catholics marry in front of a justice of the peace or a minister, this is not a valid marriage in the Church. Or, if a Catholic marries a non-Catholic (without a dispensation) in the presence of an official unauthorized by the Church, this also is not a valid marriage.

Q. 51. Are non-Catholics bound to the form of marriage?

No.

Neither baptized non-Catholics nor unbaptized persons are bound by the form of marriage. In other words, they do not have to exchange their consent in the presence of a Catholic official. In addition, a baptized Catholic who left the Church by a formal act and married after 1983 (the year the present code of law went into effect) is not bound by the form of marriage.

The Catholic Church considers marriages of baptized Protestants to be valid marriages. So if two Lutherans marry in the Lutheran church in the presence of a Lutheran minister, the Catholic Church recognizes this as a valid sacrament of marriage. If a baptized Episcopalian man marries a baptized Presbyterian woman before a justice of the peace, the Catholic Church recognizes this as a valid sacrament of marriage.

This is consistent with the Church's theological understanding of marriage. Once the two ministers (baptized Christians) have exchanged their consent, a valid, sacramental marriage comes into existence.[131] Remember, baptism is the foundation of the Christian life.[132] Indeed, how odd it would be if the Church recognized only the marriages of Roman Catholics as valid sacraments. Such an erroneous stance would deny the efficacy of the sacrament of baptism.

In addition, when two unbaptized persons marry, or a baptized and nonbaptized person marry, they bring into existence a good and natural marriage. So when two Hindus marry, the Catholic Church recognizes this as a valid marriage. It is nonsacramental in nature because neither minister is baptized, but it is nonetheless a marriage. A husband-and-wife relationship has come into existence. The same is true for the marriage of a baptized Methodist and a Buddhist, since, again, two baptized ministers are necessary for a sacramental marriage.

Once the Catholic Church recognizes a marriage as a valid sacrament or as a good and natural marriage, any question of invalidity must come before a Church tribunal if a Catholic is involved in a subsequent marriage. Since every marriage is indissoluble, the bride and groom are bound to their prior unions, regardless of a civil divorce. A tribunal investigation involving a Protestant marriage or a marriage between the unbaptized usually occurs if a subsequent marriage involves a Catholic. The divorced Protestant or unbaptized person is not free to marry a Catholic unless the first marriage can be declared invalid.

So, if two Lutherans marry and subsequently divorce, and the divorced man now wishes to marry a Catholic woman, he is not free to do so. He would only become free if the Church issued a declaration of nullity for his first marriage. On average nearly 20 percent of formal marriage cases pending before tribunals pertain to either sacramental marriages of baptized non-Catholics or good and natural marriages.

Q. 52. What is a "defect of form" case?

The law states that marriage is brought about through: (1) the consent of the bride and groom, (2) legitimately manifested, (3) by those qualified according to the law (again, the bride and the groom).[133] A **defect of form** case focuses on the second concern. It scrutinizes the legitimate

manifestation of the exchange of consent. If it is determined that the consent of the party(ies) was not legitimately manifested on the wedding day, then a valid
marriage did not come about as everyone had presumed.

Catholics are bound to follow the proper form of celebration for the marriage to be valid. The form may be defective in either of two ways: First, the ceremony was
celebrated without at least two witnesses. Second, the
priest, deacon or layperson who asked for and received the
consent of the parties was not duly qualified to do so. A tribunal investigation that seeks to determine if either of
these scenarios was operative is called a proceeding regarding a defect of form. Cases that require this type of investigation are rare.

The following is an example of a defect of form. In 1991,
two Catholics, Tom and MaryBeth, chose to marry in her
parish church in the presence of her uncle, Father Bill. Father
Bill was from the Midwest. Three months before the wedding
he had presented all of his credentials to the pastor and everything was in order. He was duly delegated to assist at the wedding as the proper official. The wedding ceremony took place
and was enjoyed by all. The legal presumption[134] was that a
valid sacramental marriage[135] had come into existence.[136]

Unfortunately, two years later the couple divorced. Tom
petitioned the Church for a declaration of nullity based on
"defect of form." It appears that after the divorce Tom was
shocked to discover that Father Bill had been suspended
from the ministry two weeks before the wedding. Therefore, he was no longer authorized to witness marriages.[137]
The priest hadn't told anyone because he was embarrassed
by these circumstances.

The tribunal investigation discovered that this was
indeed the case. Since the Church official lacked the
authority to assist at the union, the marriage was declared
null by reason of a defect of form. There was a wedding,
but not a valid marriage.

Q. 53. What is a "lack of form" case?

A **lack of form** case is different from a defect of form case. In a defect of form case, the form was present but defective in some manner. Conversely, in a lack of form case, the form was never present. Such a designation infers a complete lack of canonical form on the wedding day. Consequently, this type of case is also referred to as an **absence of form.**

As stated, a baptized Catholic who has not left the Church by a formal act must marry in the presence of a Church official. Unless the Catholic has been dispensed from it, the form of marriage is required for validity.[138] If a Catholic is not married in the presence of a priest or deacon on the wedding day, then the form of marriage has not been followed. The Church does not recognize the union as a valid marriage.

For example, if two baptized Catholics decide to marry in the presence of a justice of the peace, instead of a priest, they have not observed the form of marriage. Similarly, if a Catholic marries a non-Catholic in the presence of a non-Catholic minister (without a dispensation), the Catholic has not observed the form of marriage. By choosing not to observe the proper form of marriage, these individuals have chosen not to have their unions recognized as valid marriages by the Church. Their union has no effects in Church law; in other words, the Church does not consider them to be husband and wife.

A lack of form case is not judicial in nature, but, rather, administrative. In judicial cases the legal presumption is that the marriage in question is valid.[139] As there is no such presumption of validity in a lack of form case,[140] there is no presumption in law to overturn. Documents can prove that party(ies) legally bound to follow the form of marriage did not marry in accord with the requisite form. Since they omitted the proper form, the marriage was never valid in the Church. Since there is no valid marriage, neither party is therefore bound to the union. They are free to marry anyone, at any time, in the Church (within the confines of Church law).

A lack of form case is handled by different agencies in each diocese, either on the local parish level or administratively through diocesan chanceries or tribunals. The Church processes many of these cases annually. Those responsible for the process gather documents to establish that the parties did not follow the proper form of marriage on the wedding day.

The primary document is a recent baptismal certificate verifying the Catholic baptism of at least one of the parties. This substantiates that at least one party was bound by law to follow the proper form of marriage. It also verifies that the civil marriage in question was never subsequently validated, or blessed, in a Church ceremony. In conjunction with the baptismal certificate, two civil documents are required: the marriage certificate, which verifies the officiant was not authorized by the Church to assist at the wedding, and the civil divorce decree, which indicates that the union has been civilly dissolved. After it has been established through these documents that the proper form of marriage had not been observed, either party is then free to marry in the Church.

The process required for a lack of form case is often accomplished within weeks. It thus appears unfair to many people that Catholics who don't "follow the rules" can civilly marry, divorce and then simply marry again in the Church, while Catholics who marry in the Church and then divorce are not free to do so. It's argued that these latter Catholics "followed the rules" and so must endure the process of a formal declaration of nullity, which usually takes over a year to complete, with no guarantee of the outcome. Those who followed the rules are punished, while those who violated the rules are let off easily. Where is the justice?

The justice is found in the consequences of people's actions. Catholics who marry in the Church have made a public, lifelong commitment to one another in the midst of the community of the faithful. They are bound to this commitment in Christian love. Catholics who have married outside of the Church have chosen not to acknowledge their union in the community of the faithful. They chose to violate the law and accept the consequences that the Church does not recognize or bless their union. The Church then cannot hold them bound to what they have never publicly acknowledged—a lifelong commitment to marriage.

It can appear the Church is more forgiving of those Catholics who civilly marry and divorce than of those Catholics who marry with the Church's blessing and then divorce. Yet none of this is a matter of forgiveness. Rather, it is a recognition of the public dimension of marriage. The community of the faithful recognizes the free will of individuals to live outside the union of marriage. Catholics who marry only civilly have publicly chosen not to live as husband and wife in the Church. Therefore they are not bound to a relationship that is not a marriage.

Q. 54. What happens if a couple is happily married, but it is discovered that the marriage is invalid in law?

A couple may be happily married and suddenly discover that their marriage is indeed invalid in law. Actually, this discovery of invalidity may become known to the parties, or it may only be discovered by Church authority and thus remain unknown to the parties! In either case, the marriage can be made valid in law through a process called "convalidation."[141] To convalidate a marriage means to make an invalid marriage valid. Convalidation gives legal force, sanction and recognition to the marriage.

There are two types of convalidation. If one or both of the parties are "aware" of the invalidity, the marriage is made valid by means of "simple convalidation."[142] *This process requires the renewal of consent by at least one of the parties.* If one or both of the parties are "unaware" of the invalidity, the marriage is made valid by means of **retroactive convalidation,** also called the **sanation** of the marriage.[143] *This option does not require the renewal of consent by either party.*

Simple convalidation:

A couple may discover that their marriage has been invalid since their wedding day due to at least one of the following reasons: (1) the existence of an impediment that had rendered them unqualified in law to give consent, (2) a defect of their consent or (3) a defect of the form required for marriage. If the parties are happily married and realize that any one of these defects existed on the wedding day, they may choose simply to convalidate the marriage. Again, this means that they choose to make their invalid marriage valid. The law specifies how this is to be done in each situation.

If the party's (ies') consent from the original wedding ceremony needs to be convalidated because a diriment impediment existed on the wedding day, the impediment must first cease to exist. Then, the party or parties who were aware of its existence must acknowledge the invalidity of their union and make a new act of consent.[144] If convalidation is required because there was a defect of consent on the wedding day, then the party whose consent was defective must acknowledge the invalidity and give new consent.[145] If convalidation is required because of a defect of form on the wedding day, both parties must acknowledge invalidity and place new consent to bring about a valid marriage.

The legal intricacies of this process are certainly complex. However, the process makes sense. It can certainly happen that something was awry on the wedding day that later needs to be rectified. Once rectified, the marriage is then made valid in law by the party's (ies') renewal of consent. A valid marriage then comes into existence at the moment of this renewal.

Retroactive convalidation:

The second process that renders an invalid marriage valid is retroactive convalidation, or sanation, which is granted by Church authority for serious reasons. The legal theory behind this concept is more intricate than simple convalidation. In this instance there is no need for a renewal of consent by the parties, because their consent on the wedding day is not called into question.

Yet even though the consent was not defective, the legal manifestation of consent on the wedding day was defective, thus rendering the marriage invalid. The parties may or may not be aware of the legal defect.[146] Such defects occurring on the wedding day include: (1) an undispensed impediment that rendered the parties unqualified in law to place consent, (2) the couple did not observe the proper canonical form of marriage or (3) a defect of form.[147]

This process affirms Church teaching that the consent of the parties makes a marriage, and that no human power can supply this consent.[148] The use of a retroactive convalidation presumes that the consent of the parties was not defective in any manner on the wedding day.[149] Put simply, the couple still considers themselves married when the favor (sanation) is granted.[150] When the sanation is granted, the invalid marriage becomes valid in law from the day of the wedding ceremony; hence the term *retroactive convalidation.*[151]

Retroactive convalidation has many pastoral applications in serious situations. Suppose a Catholic woman is happily married to a non-Catholic Christian, but he has a real hatred for the Church. His hatred was so intense that he demanded that the wedding ceremony had be held outside the Church. There were no permissions granted for this because the non-Catholic refused to see the local priest. Since there was no dispensation from canonical form, the marriage is invalid. The marriage could be convalidated retroactively for the well-being of the Catholic who wishes to receive holy communion but cannot, because she is living in a union not recognized by the Church. The Catholic's request for the retroactive convalidation would be granted so that she could actively participate in the sacramental life of the Church.

Another instance in which the favor of sanation may be given involves a situation in which the parties are unaware of the invalidity of their marriage. Suppose a priest neglects to apply for a dispensation from an impediment so that a particular couple can marry validly. Further suppose that the couple is unaware of this and that the wedding ceremony is held despite the fact that they are unqualified by law to give consent. The marriage is invalid because the dispensation from the impediment was not granted. However, the marriage could be retroactively convalidated without either party knowing that this negligence had occurred. The granting of the favor in this instance would prevent the scandal involved if the circumstances of the priest's negligence became known.

However, no matter what the circumstances, it is absolutely required that the consent of the parties perdures at the time of the sanation, since consent makes marriage.

PART V:

The Tribunal and Court Officials

In the film adaptation of L. Frank Baum's, The Wizard of Oz, Dorothy approaches the Great and Wonderful Wizard with palpable fear, trepidation and hope. The grandeur of the hall heightens her fear! The unknown sounds and voices deepen her trepidation! And a dread that her request and those of her friends will be denied almost causes her to lose hope! Many who approach the tribunal can identify with that scene as well as with Dorothy's emotions.

Fear of the unknown is a disturbing thing. Since the work of the tribunal is often mystifying to people, their fears are understandable. However, a knowledge of the Church's court system should alleviate this fear of the unknown.

Q. 55. What is a tribunal; what are its different levels?

The tribunal is the name given to Church courts. The name is derived from the word "tribune," a raised platform upon which is placed the seat of a judge. The tribunal, or court, renders judgments at the request of and on behalf of people seeking justice. Judicial trials are undertaken in the Church's courts to pursue or vindicate rights, to declare legal facts or to impose penalties.[152] In regard to petitions concerning the validity of marriage, the *Catechism of the Catholic Church* states: "...the Church, after an examination of the situation by the competent Church tribunal, can declare the nullity of [the] marriage...."[153]

All of the Christian faithful have access to the courts to vindicate and defend their rights.[154] In fact, anyone, whether baptized or not, can bring a marriage case before the Church.[155] In actual practice diocesan tribunals are involved primarily with marriage cases. Any case brought before a Church court is carefully regulated by the Church's laws on trial procedures.[156]

There are three levels of Church courts in law: the first is usually in the diocese at the diocesan tribunal;[157] the second is normally regional (a region comprises a number of dioceses),

113

and it is usually titled the Court of Appeal;[158] the third level is in the Vatican and is made up of the tribunals of the Holy See.[159] There are two courts at this last level. The tribunal of the Roman Rota is the highest court of appeal in the Church. The Supreme Tribunal of the Apostolic Signatura has universal oversight for the judicial structures of the Church. The Apostolic Signatura is a type of department of justice for the Church. For example, it assists the bishop in addressing any concerns over the administration of justice in his tribunal. Cases are processed in the Church within this trilevel judicial structure.

Q. 56. What is the role of the bishop over the diocesan court?

The bishop is the chief judge of the diocese. The notions of the bishop as a judge and a system of Church courts concerned with judicial matters often sound foreign to people. Yet, they are essential elements of the power of governance within the Church.

The Church's governance is similar to the notion of governance on the federal level in the United States. There are three branches of federal government; executive, legislative and judicial. These branches are separate, though interrelated. Different people serve in the different branches of government; for example, the president serves in the executive branch, members of Congress serve in the legislative branch and the members of the Supreme Court serve in the judicial branch.

The power of governance in the Church exists within these same categories, but the categories are not separated among different people. The bishop has all three powers of governance attached to his office. He exercises governance in each sphere: executive, legislative and judicial, in accord with the norm of law. Only he can create laws (legislate); however, he can delegate his executive authority to those who minister in chanceries, and his judicial authority to those who minister in tribunals.[160]

The diocesan tribunal is the court of the bishop; as such, the bishop has chief oversight for it.[161] The tribunal is composed of judicial personnel, that is, judges, advocates, defenders of the bond of marriage and others. The judicial vicar directs the diocesan court, and in larger dioceses he is often assisted by an associate judicial vicar. These vicars serve as presiding judges on cases that are decided by a college, or panel, of either three or five judges. The defender of the bond of marriage acts according to the title of that office. He or she defends the bond of the marriage that has been brought into question. Procurators represent and act on behalf of the parties in the case—the spouses—while advocates ensure that the rights of the spouses are upheld. All of these officials exercise their judicial functions in accord with the Church's laws.

Q. 57. Can any Church court hear any marriage case?

No.

A court has jurisdiction, or competence, over marriage cases only under certain circumstances specified in law. For instance, the Holy See reserves to itself the right to hear cases concerning the heads of State, and it may reserve other cases as well.[162] This is understandable, since immense pressure could be brought to bear on local judges if a head of state petitioned the local court for a declaration of nullity.

For those cases not reserved to the Holy See, the law specifies four circumstances under which a lower court may accept a case. The lower court renders the first decision, and so it is called the Court of First Instance. This court is competent to hear a case if it is the diocesan court: (1) where the marriage occurred, (2) where the respondent lives, (3) where the petitioner lives or (4) where most of the testimonies will be collected.[163] The last two options concerning a court's jurisdiction have certain provisions attached that the two former do not. Any one of the four options is available; one does not take precedence over the others. Since the matter of jurisdiction can be complex, the following case study may help.

A CASE: Frank and Dolly were married in Boston. They are divorced and Frank is considering a petition for a declaration of nullity. Dolly presently lives in Dallas and Frank lives in San Francisco. The majority of his witnesses for the tribunal investigation live in Chicago. When deciding upon the diocese in which to submit his petition for a declaration of nullity, Frank has a number of options regarding competent tribunals: Boston, Dallas, San Francisco or Chicago.

First, he may petition the Boston tribunal to hear the case. This court is competent to do so, as it is the tribunal of the diocese where the marriage took place. In law, the place of the contract always has jurisdiction to handle a case.

Second, he may petition Dolly's tribunal in Dallas. This court is competent because it is the court of the diocese where the respondent resides. This specification of competence allows the respondent ease of access to the court. Conversely, it emphasizes that the burden of proof concerning the invalidity of marriage rests with the petitioner.

Third, Frank may petition the diocesan tribunal of San Francisco, the diocese of his place of residence. This option, however, is more complicated. There are two provisions that must be met before this tribunal may accept the case. The *first provision* is that both Frank and Dolly live within the same bishops' conference. For those living in the United States this means the fifty states, the District of Columbia and some, though not all, of the territories; for example, Puerto Rico is not included. So, if Dolly left Dallas for New Delhi when Frank decides to petition, he cannot apply to San Francisco. Since she no longer resides in the territory of the same episcopal conference, the San Francisco tribunal is not an option. The *second provision* stipulates that the respondent's judicial vicar must give his consent to the petitioner's judicial vicar after consultation with the respondent. So the judicial vicar of Dallas must contact Dolly about Frank's petition. If he gives San Francisco his consent, the case is adjudicated there. Should he refuse to give consent, the San Francisco tribunal cannot accept the case. Both provisions underscore the law's concern to safeguard the rights of the respondent in the processing of a case.

Fourth, Frank may petition the tribunal of Chicago to hear the case, as this is where most of the witnesses live. This makes sense since a good deal of case work revolves around the collection of the testimony. However, again, the law stipulates *one provision* for competence in this situation. The respondent's judicial vicar must give his consent after he has contacted the respondent regarding any objections. So the judicial vicar of Dallas must contact Dolly about Frank's petition. He may give his consent to Chicago only after he has asked Dolly whether she has any objections to the case being heard in Chicago. Again, the burden of proof is on Frank. Dolly should not be disadvantaged because of the distance from Dallas to Chicago. As an aside, the stipulation that both parties live in the same bishop's conference does not apply in this instance, as it does in the one above. So if Dolly is living in Paris, Frank may still petition Chicago.

The issue of the respondent's judicial vicar giving consent in options 3 and 4 should not discourage a petitioner from petitioning either of these courts. The issue of consent is handled with ease between tribunals. Courts work together to strive to protect the interests of all the parties involved.

Q. 58. Who are the judges?

The diocesan bishop is the chief judge in the diocese, given his judicial power of governance. However, in view of all his responsibilities, it is rare in the United States for the bishop to preside as a judge in a marriage case. Thus, it is very unlikely that a petitioner and respondent would have the bishop decide their case. Instead, the law requires the bishop to appoint a judicial vicar to assist in the judicial governance of the diocese. The law stipulates that the judicial vicar must be a priest. The judicial vicar serves on the court as a presiding judge in virtue of his office. In addition to this official, the bishop also appoints others to the office of judge to facilitate the judicial workings of the diocese.

Judges on the tribunal may be clerics—bishops, priests or deacons. With the permission of the bishops' conference, they may also be laypersons, both men and women.[164] This permission has been given in the United States. In many dioceses our courts are comprised of judges who are clerics, women and men religious and lay women and men. Collectively, the tribunals of the United States have husbands, wives, priests, religious sisters, deacons, religious brothers, single men and single women serving as judges. The law requires that every judge is to have a degree in canon law; each is also to have a good reputation in the community.[165] Given the seriousness of the judge's task, the law demands that a judge be an individual of steadfast character and established expertise.

A judge decides a case as either a single judge or as a member of a panel of three or five judges.[166] If the case is handled by a single judge, the law stipulates that the judge must be a cleric.[167] Panels are normally comprised of three judges; it is rare for a marriage case to be assigned to a panel of five judges. These three judges form a "college," with one member as the presiding judge and the other two members as collegiate judges. Two of the three members must be clerics, while the third may be a layperson.[168] The panel constitutes a college, and its decision is based on a majority vote at the time of judgment.

Judges are assigned to cases by rotation.[169] Yet, in order to guarantee impartiality and the integrity of the tribunal system, the law obliges judges to excuse themselves from hearing any case in which they may have a personal interest.[170] This would include cases of relatives, close friends or adversaries, and cases that hold the possibility for financial loss or gain for the judge.[171]

Even though petitioners and respondents cannot choose the judges they wish to hear their case, they may object to a particular judge who is assigned by rotation. This objection is made to the judicial vicar. If the objection is against the judicial vicar, the matter is referred to the bishop. If the objection is upheld, the official is removed immediately from the case.[172] This is done because the search for truth demands impartiality. Every effort should be made to see that the integrity of the judiciary is never compromised.

Q. 59. What is the role of the judge?

A judge has extensive responsibilities in law, but the primary duty is to hear and decide cases. He or she is to ensure that the procedural rights of parties are protected and that cases are decided as quickly as possible, preferably within a year.[173] The judge may exercise judicial discretion regarding various actions during the tribunal investigation; for example, he may extend the time limits under which party(ies) are to perform actions,[174] or he may withhold some testimonies from the parties for serious reasons.[175] Ultimately, he evaluates all of the submitted testimonies in light of the Church's law and the writings of jurists in his or her impartial search for truth.

The ultimate responsibility of a judge is to issue a sentence that decides the case. The judge pronounces judgment on the nullity of a marriage in a "formal sentence." The sentence must clearly settle the controversy.[176] It contains an orderly and logical argument that explains how the decision was determined. If the case is decided in the affirmative, the sentence demonstrates why the marriage is null in view of the various testimonies and in light of the law. If the case is decided in the negative, the sentence demonstrates the opposite. A single judge writes his own sentence. A college has one of the judges write the opinion on behalf of the others.[177]

The opinions of numerous judges decide the final outcome of a case. Every sentence from a Court of First Instance moves to a Court of Second Instance, that is, the Appeal Court. The minimum number of judges required to decide a case is four (one diocesan court judge and three appellate judges); normally, the maximum number is six (three diocesan court judges and three appellate judges). The number of judges may be higher if the various panels are comprised of five judges or if there are two trials on the appellate level. Regardless, the final decision regarding validity or invalidity is made by numerous judges.

Q. 60. What is the role of an advocate?

The bishop appoints advocates to his court. Advocates safeguard the rights of the petitioner and respondent by working on their behalf. This official works before the court and, as such, is not an instrument of the court. An advocate may be a man or woman at least eighteen years of age with a good reputation in the community, and regarded as an "expert" in canon law, though an academic degree is not required. This person should also preferably be a Catholic.[178] Most tribunals have a list of approved advocates, and these individuals are available to the parties.[179] If a party wishes to appoint an advocate who is not on the approved list, this request may be made to the bishop.

The advocate is appointed to the case by the party, not the court.[180] Normally, the petitioner and respondent appoint their advocates from the approved diocesan list. This usually occurs within the initial phase of the tribunal investigation. It is accomplished by the parties signing an official decree of appointment called a *mandate*. This commissions the advocate to work on their behalf. These appointments are optional. Neither the petitioner nor the respondent is required to commission an advocate.[181]

The advocate has various roles throughout the tribunal investigation. He may be present when the parties, witnesses or experts give testimony,[182] and he may inspect all of the testimony once it has been submitted.[183] However, one of his most important roles is to write a "legal brief" on behalf of his party and submit this to the judge(s) for consideration.[184] By means of the brief, the advocate is to exert all possible efforts to emphasize everything relative to his client's position in the case. Thus, the advocate for the petitioner will strive to prove the nullity of the marriage for the petitioner, while the advocate for an opposed respondent will endeavor to refute any suggestion that the marriage is invalid.

This is not to infer that the client's interests supersede the search for truth. As the judge's main duty is the impartial search for truth, so too is it the duty of the advocate. An advocate cannot induce parties or witnesses to lie to the court, nor can he employ fraud or dishonesty in his arguments to the court. He must always act according to the right dictates of his conscience. The search for justice is the search for truth. Therefore, deceptive, though skillful, argumentation has no place in a tribunal investigation regarding marriage.

Q. 61. What is the role of a procurator?

Another name for a procurator is a proxy. This court official is commissioned by the petitioner or respondent to perform judicial acts in his or her name. This official is a person's personal representative to the court.[185] Like the advocate, the procurator works before the court, and, as such, is not an instrument of the court. Many tribunals have a list of approved procurators; these legal representatives are often paid by the tribunal and available to the parties.[186] A procurator may be a man or a woman. The only legal qualifications for this official are that he or she is at least eighteen years of age and has a good reputation.

As with the appointment of the advocate, the petitioner and respondent must commission the procurator to act on their behalf by virtue of a signed mandate.[187] However, this appointment is optional; neither the petitioner nor the respondent must commission a procurator.[188] In some instances, the party's advocate may also be commissioned to serve as the procurator. The official is then known as the procurator-advocate.

The procurator may be present at the examination of the witnesses.[189] Yet the primary role of the procurator is to perform specified legal actions on behalf of the party at different phases of the investigation.[190] The principal action a procurator can perform on behalf of the party is to appeal the judge's sentence.[191] Even though the procurator works on behalf of a party, like other officials of the court, his or her ultimate interest is the truth.

Q. 62. What is the role of the defender of the bond of marriage?

Unlike the party's advocate or procurator, the defender of the bond of marriage is an officer of the court who acts on behalf of the court. The defender is bound by office to propose and clarify everything that can be reasonably adduced **against** a declaration of nullity.[192] He "defends" the validity of the "bond of marriage" that is in question; hence the title of the office.

It is the responsibility of the diocesan bishop to appoint a defender to his tribunal. As with judges, advocates and procurators, defenders of the bond of marriage may be clerics, women and men religious and lay women and men. The law stipulates that the defender should have a good reputation, hold a degree in canon law and exhibit both prudence and a zeal for justice.[193] Husbands, wives, priests, religious sisters, deacons, religious brothers, single men and women are capable of serving as defenders on tribunals.

The defender of the bond of marriage has various roles throughout the tribunal investigation. He or she ensures that the rights of both parties are upheld. The defender also examines the testimonies in a case, pointing out to the judge(s) contradictions between testimonies or gaps between the testimony of one person vis-à-vis another person. He highlights for the judge facts or statements that undermine or weaken the petition for nullity. He may suggest that the judge question the parties and witnesses about specific matters;[194] he may also be present when the witnesses are examined.[195] If the case is decided in the affirmative, the defender may appeal this decision.[196]

After all of the testimony in the case has been presented, the principal role of the defender is to argue reasonably for the validity of the "bond of marriage."[197] This is principally accomplished through the defender's written legal brief, which is submitted to the judge(s).[198] As with the other officials in the tribunal investigation, the ultimate goal of the defender's activity is the search for truth. Therefore, he is not obliged to defend the marriage bond in question at any cost. In the interest of truth and after a diligent, accurate and conscientious examination of all of the testimonies, the defender may find no reasonable objection to the petition for nullity. The defender does not have to devise an artificial argument for validity in a case that clearly suggests invalidity. Rather, he may simply state he has no reasonable objections. Ultimately, the defender of the bond of marriage serves the search for truth.

Q. 63. What is the role of an "expert" witness?

An expert witness is someone with a technical knowledge or skill who utilizes his or her area of expertise to aid the judge in the search for truth.[199] More often than not, experts in tribunal investigations are psychiatrists, psychologists or other professionals in the field of mental health. They usually offer the court professional opinions regarding a party's consent on the wedding day. Cases heard on the grounds of a lack of due reason, a grave lack of discretion of judgment or a lack of due competence often utilize the expertise of such experts. In addition, cases concerning impotence normally warrant the use of an expert as well, for example, a urologist or gynecologist.[200]

It is up to the judge to decide if an expert's analysis is needed in a case.[201] He may decide this on his own, or he may call on an expert at the request of one of the parties.[202] The judge may ask a party to see one of the court's experts for a professional opinion; or a party may request that the court contact his or her private counselor.[203] Many individuals have undergone psychological therapy; this is especially true before or after a divorce. Their established relationship with a professional in the mental health field may be of assistance to them during the tribunal investigation. It is the prerogative of the judge to accept or reject the party's request for their own counselor to give testimony.[204]

Many tribunals have professional experts associated with the court. This is one way of ensuring that the expert assesses individuals from the perspective of a Christian anthropology that situates the essence and nature of humankind within the creative power of God. If the expert is to assist the judge, and the judge is to properly evaluate the expert's opinion, both must basically have a similar starting point in regard to marriage. The Church holds that marriage is willed by God; as such, it is a vocation. Two people bring about the marital community of life and love through a mutual self-giving. This involves renunciation and sacrifice as well as joy and happiness.

If an expert rejects the Church's understanding of marriage, that person's evaluation may be of little value to the judge. In essence the starting points of the expert and the judge are so far apart that the interchange will be of little value. For instance, an expert working outside of a Christian anthropology may equate the sacrifices of marriage with a person's sense of unhappiness. He or she may then conclude that the unhappy spouse lacked grave discretion of judgment at the time of consent, while experts who hold to a Christian anthropology will evaluate the circumstances of the case in regard to their own professional competence and also be attentive to the Christian message concerning the vision of human nature and of matrimony. These experts will be able to evaluate if the unhappy spouse was incapable of marriage or simply chose to reject the obligations of marriage.

The expert is to offer a professional opinion regarding the consent of the party(ies) on the wedding day. The judge will specify the individual points on which the expert's services should focus. The professional's report should be a reasoned opinion that establishes a professional diagnosis regarding an infirmity or emotional disorder. Its purpose is to identify psychological factors that may have affected the party(ies) leading up to the exchange of consent on the wedding day.[205]

The law specifies that the judge is to weigh the expert's conclusions in light of other circumstances in the case. It is for the judge alone to decide in favor of nullity; this is not the prerogative of the expert. However, when the judge issues his sentence, he is to give reasons as to why he accepted or rejected the expert's conclusions.[206]

It is the responsibility of the parties to pay any professional expenses incurred through the use of experts,[207] but the expert's report is for the judge, not the parties. As such, the parties do not have the right to review the report. The report is intended to aid the judge in his or her determination regarding the petition for nullity.

PART VI:

Participating in the Tribunal Investigation

Q. 64. Who is the petitioner?

A tribunal investigation cannot begin unless a person brings a case before a judge.[208] In regard to marriage, either spouse has the right to "petition" the Church for a declaration of nullity.[209] The petitioner is the spouse who initiates the case before the court. It is more correct to speak of the petitioner as the "plaintiff," since the petitioner is asking for a right, not a favor.

As a plaintiff, the spouse is seeking to have his or her marriage declared invalid. The law presumes that the petitioner is married, regardless of a civil divorce. However, the petitioner believes that the marriage is invalid and thus contends that he or she is unmarried, that is, single. The petitioner's question concerning the validity of the marriage ultimately questions his or her legal status in the Church. If the marriage is declared null, the parties are not bound to a union; both parties would be legally unmarried, and so are free to marry at any time.

Due to Church/State issues as well as concerns over civil litigation for alienation of affection, most tribunals in the United States will not accept a petition unless there has been a civil divorce. As such any divorced person has the right to petition the Church for a declaration of nullity.

That is quite distinct from saying that any divorced individual has a right to a declaration of nullity. This is not the case. At times the decision is in the affirmative; at other times it is in the negative. Thousands of men and women bring petitions for nullity to the Church each year in the United States. Women constitute a slightly higher percent of petitioners. No one is penalized for being well known, nor for being unknown. Everyone is accorded the same procedural rights and treated justly in accord with the norm of law.[210]

Tribunals across the country vary in the manner in which they accept petitions for a declaration of nullity. A petitioner either relates the history of the marital relationship to the court in written form or through verbal testimony. This history includes a complete account of the family backgrounds of each party, their courtship, wedding, marital life and separation(s). In view of this testimony the court will determine if the petition should be accepted and on what ground(s) the petitioner has cause for a case. The petitioner is then requested to sign a "formal petition," in Latin, *libellus,* to initiate the investigation.[211] As the case proceeds, the petitioner may be asked to clarify certain points or expand on areas that need elaboration.

The petitioner may appoint an advocate and a procurator to assist him or her during the tribunal process;[212] tribunals facilitate these appointments. In addition, the petitioner may also perform a number of specific actions during the process, for instance, a review of material at the time of the publication of the acts and of the sentence (questions and answers on these actions follow below). These actions and others must be accomplished within specified time periods so that the entire process is not delayed. Finally, when a decision is rendered, the petitioner may appeal the final result if he or she is displeased with the outcome.

Q. 65. Who is the respondent?

The respondent is the other spouse to the marriage, who is notified by the court of the petition and asked to "respond." The respondent must be contacted, so the petitioner must present a current address or a "care of" address for their spouse. It is the tribunal's responsibility to contact the respondent about the proceedings; the petitioner is not obliged to do so. However, ex-spousal hostilities after a divorce can be exacerbated by "unannounced" tribunal proceedings. So if the parties are on good terms it may be prudent for the petitioner to inform the respondent ahead of time.

Once the respondent has been contacted (the legal term is "cited"), he or she has a number of explicit options that are quite proactive. He (or she) responds to the citation and indicates that he is: (1) opposed to the petition, (2) in favor of the petition or (3) indifferent to the petition and wishes no further contact. In the first two instances the respondent should actively participate in the process. In the last instance the respondent effectively waives his or her rights throughout the investigation, with the exception of choosing to appeal the final sentence.

Like the petitioner, the respondent may appoint an advocate and a procurator for assistance throughout the tribunal process;[213] again, tribunals facilitate these appointments. The respondent, like the petitioner, may also perform a number of specific actions during the process, for instance, a review of material at the time of the publication of the acts and of the sentence. These actions and others must be accomplished within the time periods specified in the law. Finally, when a decision is rendered, the respondent may appeal the final decision if he or she is displeased with the outcome.

The respondent also has an implicit option that is passive. He may choose to be uncooperative with the investigation by issuing no response to the citation. Again, the law requires the respondent be cited. This is normally done through the United States postal service. Many tribunals ensure the receipt of citation by the use of certified mail. The postal receipt verifies the reception of the citation.

If a respondent does not respond to the court within the specified time of receipt, the judge may declare him absent from the proceedings.[214] This decree of illegitimate absence frees the judge to omit all of the parts the respondent would play if he or she were participating in the process. A failure to reply to the citation presumes that the respondent has relinquished any right to future correspondence from the court. The only possible exception would be an appeal of the final sentence. However, in order to exercise this right of appeal, the respondent must be able to show the court that there was good reason for not appearing before this end point in the process.[215]

Occasionally, a petitioner will claim the respondent is unlocatable. It is rare today for a person simply to disappear. More often than not, the petitioner has had no contact with the other spouse for a long period of time, or hostilities between the two are high. The petitioner may not want to have anything to do with the other party. However, these are not reasons for the court to dismiss the required citation. The citation must be done. Yet, one cannot deny the possibility that the respondent is indeed unable to be located. The petitioner should prove to the court the various avenues that he or she has undertaken to find the respondent, even though these measures have proved fruitless. In this rare situation an officer of the court, called a "legal representative," is to act in the respondent's place.[216]

Q. 66. What is the role of witnesses in the investigation?

A witness is an individual who has been summoned by the court to testify to questions posed by the judge. The testimony of a witness is one source of proof to the court regarding the case.[217] Both the petitioner and the respondent can supply the court with names of witnesses.[218] In addition, either party can object to a witness proposed by the other spouse, with the decision to exclude a witness belonging to the judge.[219]

It is also the responsibility of the judge to curb an excessive number of witnesses.[220] Most tribunals generally limit the number of witnesses that each spouse may present to three as a minimum and five as a maximum; a specific case, however, may warrant more than five witnesses. A valuable witness is one who knew the parties before and after the wedding day. Family members—parents, brothers, sisters, aunts, uncles and cousins—often provide very useful material to the court. Childhood or school friends can also elaborate on the parties' developmental years, which is beneficial information to the court. Individuals who knew the spouses during their courtship and married life are also useful witnesses.

Most petitioners and respondents feel awkward about naming witnesses. They believe it is an imposition on the persons' time and often drags up sad memories from their past. These hesitations are usually correct. It is uncomfortable to testify before a court on such serious, complex and personal matters. However, a petition for nullity can usually only be proven or adequately opposed through the testimonies of witnesses.

The operative legal presumption is that the marriage in question is valid. This presumption will yield to contrary evidence only if such evidence exists. So the petitioner needs to present witnesses to substantiate his or her claim. The opposed respondent should also present witnesses to counter the position of the petitioner and support the presumed validity of the marriage. Again, the presumption of validity will yield to nullity if the testimonies are convincing. Respondent witnesses add the weight of their testimonies to the process. The respondent should not waive his or her right to the naming of witnesses.

The law states that anyone who is not expressly excluded by law can serve as a witness.[221] Those excluded are children under fourteen years of age and priests who have acted as confessors to either party through the sacrament of penance.[222] Other witnesses can be exempted from giving testimony; for instance, anyone who is bound by professional secrecy, such as bishops, priests and deacons, as well as medical and legal professionals. In addition, anyone who fears a loss of reputation or dangerous reprisals by giving testimony, not only to themselves but also to anyone close to them, can be exempted.[223] The judge decides this matter of exemption.[224]

Witnesses are examined individually, not as a group.[225] The examination of a witness is conducted by the judge or duly appointed court official either through oral or written testimonies.[226] Oral testimonies are usually taken at the tribunal office. The parties may not be present at this examination, though their advocates and procurators may be there.[227]

Aside from the taking of oral testimonies, some tribunals gather witness testimonies though written affidavits. This may be necessary due to a shortage of court personnel or because the diocese may be so large territorially that witnesses are unable to travel to the tribunal. Affidavits are usually less time consuming for the court. Some tribunals have discovered that many more affidavits can be obtained in the time that it takes to acquire just a few verbal testimonies.

Whether by oral testimony or written affidavits, it is understood that the witness is to testify to the whole truth and only the truth.[228] It is the responsibility of the judge to evaluate the reliability and weight of the testimony. At the outset the judge should consider the good reputation of the witness. He should then ascertain whether the witness is testifying from personal firsthand knowledge or from opinion, rumor or hearsay. Is the witness credible, or does the testimony appear inconsistent or uncertain? Does the testimony of the witness find corroboration in the testimony of the other witnesses or other sources of proof? The judge must probe the testimony to discover the truth. Witnesses will offer testimonies of varying weight.

Q. 67. What are the stages of a tribunal investigation concerning marriage?

There are five stages to a tribunal investigation concerning the validity of a marriage. The stages are: (1) the introduction of the case, (2) the collection of testimonies, (3) the review of testimonies and the discussion among the court officials, (4) the decision of the judge(s) and (5) the appeal process. The first four stages are in the First Instance Court and take approximately one year.[229] The last stage takes place in the Second Instance Court. This stage can take anywhere from one to six months, depending on the type of appeal and the court before which it has been brought.[230] (The time estimations that follow are changeable. They will differ significantly among tribunals, depending on the volume of cases handled by each tribunal and the availability of trained full-time and part-time personnel.)

The Introduction: A spouse initiates a case to the court through the submission of a "formal petition." The tribunal officials determine the nature of the case. It may focus on the consent of the bride and groom, or the legitimate manifestation of that consent, or the parties' qualifications to place consent. The judge determines the court's jurisdiction, the petitioner's standing in court and whether the case has merit.

Then the "citation of the respondent" occurs, and the judge fixes the legal ground(s) on which the case is to proceed. This initial stage can take approximately two to three months.

The Collection of Testimonies: The petitioner and respondent present their respective declarations. The witnesses that they have named are contacted for their testimonies.

Expert witnesses may be called, such as mental health professionals or medical doctors. Documents may be requested, such as counselors' reports, hospital admissions paperwork or criminal records. This stage usually takes the greatest amount of time—anywhere from two to six months.

The Review of Testimonies and the Discussion among Court Officials: After the testimonies have been collected, the "publication of the acts" occurs. After this publication the party(ies) may propose additional proofs. When the parties have nothing more to add or their time to do so has expired, the collection of proofs is considered concluded. Then the parties' advocates and the defender of the bond of marriage present legal arguments to the judge(s). Traditionally, these arguments are in the form of written legal briefs. However, this phase may also be accomplished through oral argumentation. Through either means the officials highlight certain facts and circumstances of the case for the judge(s), so that the judge(s) may render a well-founded decision. This stage can take from one to three months.

The Decision of the Judge(s): The judge(s) then render a decision by means of a judicial sentence. The sentence states the basic facts of the case, such as an identification of the parties and the relevant facts and dates surrounding the marriage. It also presents the law and jurisprudence upon which the case is decided in the affirmative or in the negative. Lastly, it argues the facts of the case in light of the law. Once the sentence is issued by the judge(s), the "publication of the sentence" occurs. This stage can take approximately one month.

The Appeal Process: All judgments rendered in the Court of First Instance are forwarded or appealed to the next tribunal level, the Court of Second Instance. Three separate actions can be taken on the appellate level. First, there is a mandatory review of a First Instance affirmative decision, which takes one to two months. Second, there may be a complaint by a party over the procedural correctness of the case. It may take two to three months to address this complaint. Finally, either party may formally appeal a decision with which they disagree. Formal appeals can last six months.

If the sentence of the First Instance Court is confirmed by the judges of the Second Instance Court, then the decision is usually final.

Q. 68. What is a "formal petition" for nullity?

In order to contest the validity of a marriage, a spouse must present the request, or plea, before a judge.[231] This plea is made by means of a "formal petition."[232] That is why the person who initiates the case is referred to as the petitioner. The formal petition is often referred to by its Latin designation, *libellus,* which literally translates as a "little book," meaning "something in writing." The plea sets out in writing the controversy that is brought before the judge.

In actual practice, tribunals assist individuals who wish to petition the Church for a declaration of nullity. The manner of assistance varies from place to place, but it is normally accomplished through the cooperation of parish ministers, regional advocates or tribunal personnel. This usually involves an informal preliminary investigation before the petition is drawn up. This investigation is not intended to determine the merits of the case, but only whether a petition may possibly establish a case for nullity.

The formal petition states the names of the spouses, the ground(s) upon which the case should be heard, the facts and proofs that will be used in general throughout the course of the investigation, the address of the respondent, the signature of the petitioner and the date the petition was submitted.[233] The information is succinctly formulated. It serves as an outline for the direction the case will take throughout the process to its completion. Without a formal petition, there can be no valid judgment.[234]

The judge will either accept or reject the petition by a decree.[235] Normally, petitions are accepted; however, this is not always the case. The petition will be rejected if the judge or tribunal lacks the jurisdiction to hear the case. It will also be rejected if the judge determines it has no basis in law, no available proofs to back it up or no foundation upon which to build a case.[236] If the petition is rejected by the judge, the petitioner has recourse to the higher authority as provided by law.[237] The higher authority will either confirm the judge's decision or overturn it.

Q. 69. What is the "citation" of the respondent?

The citation is the summons indicating to the respondent that a court action has been initiated by the petitioner. It calls for the respondent to "respond" to the petitioner's plea before the court that the marriage is invalid. This summons is issued to the respondent by the judge. The judge decides whether the respondent is to answer the summons in person or through writing.[238] Once the citation of the respondent has occurred, the trial investigation has officially begun.[239]

The citation is a crucial step in the proceedings. It affords the respondent his or her right to respond to the petitioner's plea. In effect, it provides the respondent with the right of defense.[240] If the respondent is not lawfully given this right of defense, the entire proceeding will be declared null.[241] So if the citation is omitted and the case nonetheless moves to an affirmative sentence, the sentence is rendered meaningless.[242] The sentence, not the marriage, is null because the respondent's right of defense was denied.

The law recommends that the summons should be sent to the respondent by the postal service or some other secure means. A record should be placed in the case file indicating the manner of delivery.[243] This record is important, as it substantiates the tribunal's summons. It may be necessary to produce the record if the respondent later claims that he or she was never cited. Again, such a claim, if substantiated, could nullify the proceedings.

If the respondent refuses to accept the summons, or circumvents its delivery, he or she is nonetheless regarded as having been duly cited, and the case proceeds.[244] This prevents the respondent from delaying the trial by putting it off until the timing is more convenient for him or her. Also, since postdivorce situations frequently contain high levels of animosity between the spouses, a vindictive respondent cannot hamper the investigation by simply refusing the citation.

The "formal petition" states the ground(s) upon which the petitioner's plea is brought forth, and it identifies how the case will be demonstrated by the petitioner. Normally, the "formal petition" is attached to the summons, so that the respondent has the opportunity to prepare a defense. Yet, the right of the respondent to see the petition at this introductory stage is not absolute. The judge may exercise discretion in this regard.[245]

For serious reasons the judge may decide not to reveal the "formal petition" to the respondent until after the respondent has given evidence. As stated, the "formal petition" contains the proofs by which the petitioner will demonstrate the case. Therefore, good reasons for withholding the petition would be a legitimate fear that the respondent will initiate a civil action of defamation against the petitioner or the Church, or interfere with the witnesses and other proposed proofs. If the petition is withheld, the respondent's right of defense is not lost, because the summons will contain the reasons behind the petitioner's plea. Additionally, the respondent will be given access to the "formal petition" later in the process during the Publication of the Acts.

Q. 70. What is the "Publication of the Acts"?

After all of the necessary testimonies have been collected, the judge issues a decree to the petitioner and the respondent called the "Publication of the Acts." This decree permits them and their advocates to inspect the testimonies at the tribunal. This general rule of inspection allows for the parties' right of defense. However, an exception to this rule is also stated in the law. The judge may withhold a given act from anyone "in order to avoid very serious dangers," providing the right of defense remains intact.[246]

This inspection of testimonies is one of the most sensitive components in the tribunal process. There are many values behind this law concerning a review of the materials. The primary value is the right of defense, and it is afforded to both the respondent and the petitioner.[247] Both parties should have access to what the other has said in order to defend their own positions. However, another value at stake is the right to one's good reputation and privacy.[248]

Ultimately, Church authority is entitled to regulate the exercise of persons' rights in view of the common good.[249] The judge exercises this responsibility at the time of publication. He or she is to ensure that the right of defense is offered through the review of testimony, but must also respect confidentiality, lest a person's right to a good reputation is ruined. The law does not specify under what parameters testimony is to be kept confidential. However, other canons shed some light on the matter. A judge may bind parties to an oath of secrecy in order to avoid dissension, scandal or the endangerment of a person's reputation.[250] Since marriage cases can be fiercely debated and postdivorce hostilities can remain very high, a judge should, at times, withhold information from the parties. This withholding of testimony may safeguard against acts of public scandal, dissension within the family or community and the ruination of reputations.

If testimony is withheld, the right of defense is still maintained, since the parties' advocates may perform a thorough review of the testimonies. In addition, the defender of the bond of marriage will also assess the material. This official's role is crucial, and it highlights the key focus of the investigation—the bond of marriage—not who is at fault for the failure of the relationship. The roles of these court officials vis-à-vis the petitioner and the respondent demonstrate that the "right of defense" and the "right to know" are separate.

If, after the review of the evidence, the parties wish to add more testimonies or present new witnesses, they may make their requests known to the judge. After these additional testimonies have been assembled, it is left to the judge's discretion as to whether another review of testimony by the parties is necessary.[251] When everything has been submitted, the collection of testimony is then concluded.[252]

Q. 71. What is the impact of the judge's sentence in the Court of First Instance?

The judgment, or sentence, is the legal pronouncement by the judge(s) that decides the case brought before the court by the petitioner. Yet, this single judgment, if in the affirmative, does not in itself declare that the marriage is null. A declaration of nullity is granted only after two affirmative judgments. So, after the First Instance judgment is issued, either party to the case or the defender of the bond of marriage may appeal the sentence.

The judge arrives at his or her decision with "moral certainty." This is a legal term in the Church that falls between the extremes of absolute certainty and probability. On one hand, it excludes a well-founded or reasonable doubt, and on the other hand, it admits to the possibility that the contrary may also be true. This objective judgment is based on the testimonies in the case. It cannot be based upon the judge's opinion or upon private knowledge that has come to him from outside the official acts of the case. If the judge cannot come to moral certitude about nullity, then the marriage remains valid in law. The contrary has not been established by the petitioner.[253]

The contents of the sentence must state clearly how the issue has been decided. The sentence must contain the reasons in law and fact upon which the decision was based. It is also to determine any obligations that remain for the parties to fulfill. The most obvious obligations arising from a marriage case are parents' responsibilities to children. The sentence should highlight the moral and civil obligation of parents to their children.[254] Finally, it should apportion the expenses that have been incurred in the trial.

The sentence has a formal structure. It begins by invoking the name of God and is then divided into four parts: First, the judge(s) and tribunal are identified, as well as the names and addresses of the petitioner and respondent, and the court officials assigned to the case. Second, there is a brief recital of the salient facts and the ground(s) upon which the case was investigated. The third section is the most important part. It is divided into the "dispositive" and "expositive" sections. The former states in one or two sentences the actual decision, either in the affirmative or the negative; the latter argues the facts of the case in light of Church law. The fourth section ends the sentence with the date and place, as well as the signatures of the judge(s) and a Church notary.

The judgment is to be published to the parties as soon as possible through a decree called the "Publication of the Sentence."[255] Informing the parties of the judge's sentence allows them the opportunity to appeal that decision. This is basic to a person's right of defense. The Publication of the Sentence is similar in nature to the Publication of the Acts. So similarly, if certain testimonies or facts were withheld at the time of the Publication of the Acts, they should also be withheld at this part of the process. The values at stake at that previous stage in the process are also relevant at this juncture. The parties must be informed of the actual decision at the Publication of the Sentence, while their procurators may be afforded the right to review the sentence in its entirety.[256]

At the Publication of the Sentence, both the petitioner and the respondent are to be informed of their right to appeal the sentence.[257] Either party may appeal the decision to the ordinary or extraordinary Court of Appeal, that is, the local appeal court or the Roman Rota. Again, this sentence from the Court of First Instance is NOT a declaration of nullity. It does not have the impact of a final decree of nullity. A decree of nullity is given only after two affirmative decisions, one from the First Instance Court and the other from the Second Instance Court.

Q. 72. What is the "appeal" process?

An "appeal" is recourse to a higher court against a decision given by a lower court. No marriage is actually declared null in the Church until there are two affirmative decisions. This is referred to in law as two "concordant decisions," meaning that both decisions agree on the matter concerning the same parties, the same marriage and the same grounds. This two-tier trial system originated in the Church in the mid-1700s. Pope Benedict XIV was concerned that too many annulments were being granted too easily, especially in Poland.

In order to ensure that justice was being served, Pope Benedict also instituted the office of the defender of the bond of marriage into the court structures. This court official was to argue for the "bond of marriage" in the First Instance Court and appeal an affirmative decision of this lower court to the Court of Second Instance. These procedural additions of an appeal court and an official called the defender of the bond of marriage established a type of "quality control" over the Church's judiciary.

Any decision rendered in a Court of First Instance may be appealed by (1) the parties, (2) the defender of the bond of marriage or (3) the law. First, if an opposed respondent is unhappy with an affirmative decision from the Court of First Instance, he or she has the right to lodge an appeal to a higher court. Conversely, if a petitioner is unhappy with a negative decision in the Court of First Instance, he or she also has the right to appeal. Second, the defender of the bond of marriage may appeal an affirmative sentence, even if the parties are not unhappy with the decision. Third, the law requires an appeal of every First Instance affirmative decision. Even if the parties and the defender of the bond of marriage are not opposed, the law requires that the decision must still be "reviewed" on the appellate level. So the Court of First Instance transmits the case to the Appellate Court. At the time of review, the Court of Second Instance is either to ratify the decision without delay or admit the case to the ordinary appeal process.[258]

There are two courts higher than the diocesan court in the Church's three-tier court system. They are the Regional Court, or "ordinary" court of appeals, and the Roman Rota, the "extraordinary" court of appeals. The required "review" established in law for an affirmative decision is handled by the ordinary court of appeals.[259] Most cases move through the appellate level on this review, and the process is usually accomplished within a two-month period.

Aside from the required review, cases on appeal may follow one of two other tracts. First, the case may be appealed to the ordinary appeal court; this is, in fact, the presumed court of appeal in law.[260] This appellate process is to be completed within a six-month time frame.[261] Second, the decision may also be appealed to the extraordinary court of appeals, the Roman Rota.[262] However, the party must state that this extraordinary court of appeals is his or her choice at the time of appeal, since the law presumes that the ordinary court will process the appeal.[263] In addition, parties should be apprised of the fact that having a case heard in the Vatican involves considerable expense. The party appealing is responsible for these expenses.

When a case moves from the Court of First Instance to the Court of Second Instance, for either "review" or "appeal," certain materials are forwarded to the latter court. This includes the decision of a First Instance Court, as well as the testimonies in the case and any appeals. These are sent to the Second Instance Court within twenty days of the Publication of the Sentence.[264] An appellate panel of three judges and a defender of the bond of marriage are assigned to the case.[265] The parties are apprised of the steps required in the appeal process by the Court of Second Instance.

Q. 73. What are the types of time limits in the tribunal proceedings?

In total, the tribunal investigation in the Court of First Instance should be concluded ideally within one year, and the investigation in the Court of Second Instance within six months.[266] There are time limits of lesser specification that add up to these total time frames. These are: a *legal* time limit, which is defined by the law; a *judicial* time limit, which is specified by the judge; and a *conventional* time period, which is arranged by the parties.

Parties have the right to perform certain actions throughout the investigation within these time periods. In some instances the time period to act is *peremptory,* that is, the right is lost if the deadline isn't met. Otherwise, the time period to act is *nonperemptory,* that is, the right is not lost if the deadline passes.

Generally, legal time limits that refer to the parties are peremptory, while those referring to the court are not. As stated, when a peremptory time limit is up, the right to act is lost; for example, an appeal against a judge's decision may be lodged by the petitioner or the respondent within fifteen days. An imaginary steel wall closes on this right on the sixteenth day. Peremptory legal deadlines can never be extended for any reason. However, they may be shortened on occasion at the request of the parties.[267]

Other legal time limits are nonperemptory. Again, these usually refer to actions that are to be taken by court officials. For example, if the three judges on a panel need to discuss a case a second time, they should do so within a week of the first discussion.[268] This legal deadline is nonperemptory; it may be extended by the judges. However, as a rule, the extension should not unduly prolong the case.

Finally, judicial and conventional time frames may be extended before they expire. A judge may grant a time extension at the request of the party(ies) or on his or her own, if the parties are notified. Ultimately, the judge should ensure that the case is handled expeditiously, and thus he should avoid undue postponements.[269] In addition, once all of the parties have agreed to a specified time, it may not be shortened validly without the consent of the other party.[270] This ensures equity and fairness.

There are laws that specifically deal with the proper calculation of time in a tribunal investigation.[271] More often than not, the days to act are working days; religious and civil holidays are normally not part of the calculation.[272] In practice, it is the tribunal's responsibility to inform the parties of the peremptory and nonperemptory time frames as they occur throughout the process.

Q. 74. Are there any fees associated with the processing of a case?

Yes.

The universal law of the Church has one canon that deals with judicial expenses as well as the issue of free legal aid.[273] A determination regarding actual expenditures is left to the bishop, since he is ultimately responsible for the workings of his tribunal.[274] The bishop, in consultation with the judicial vicar, decides on reasonable fees that are to be paid by the petitioner and respondent for the court's services.[275] These assessed costs are not donations to the Church. Rather, they are fees for services rendered. In most dioceses there are varying fees for differing types of cases. In some dioceses there are no fees associated with tribunal processes.

Parties may also be assessed fees for the services of court advocates, procurators, interpreters and experts.[276] Again, this will differ from tribunal to tribunal. Generally, dioceses include the costs of these court personnel in the general assessment. However, an exception to this policy may be the fee associated with experts in the mental health professions, such as psychiatrists, psychologists and clinical social workers. These individuals' fees are usually in addition to the general assessment.

Tribunals also have guidelines for free legal aid and the reduction of fees.[277] There are instances in which the parties cannot assume the nominal costs associated with a case; this does not affect the investigation. In cases of financial need the fee may be waived. Or, furthermore, if there is a need to pay in installments, the person should be accommodated. These accommodations to the parties are made by the judge.

It is important to note that the assessment of fees normally reflects only a part of the actual court expenditures. The moneys support the overall operation of the tribunal, such as salaries for professional and support staffs, computer hardware and software, office supplies, postage, building expenses and the like. Actually, in the tribunals receiving assessments, such income only covers a percentage of the actual case costs. The dioceses assume the rest of the cost. No tribunal supplies for its annual operating expenses solely through the assessment of fees.[278] Some tribunals in the United States do not assess the parties any fees. In these places the diocese fully subsidizes its tribunal.

As with the executive and legislative dimensions of the

Church's governance, the judicial system does not exist to generate money, and, in fact, it does not.

Q. 75. Why are the proceedings confidential to those outside of the case?

Trials in Church law are not public events. They are governed by laws of secrecy or strict confidentiality. This is not to imply that the parties involved in the case have secrets kept from them; the parties are fully informed of the proceedings in order to protect their rights of defense. Rather, the trials themselves are kept out of the public spotlight. Since individuals have a right to their privacy and good reputation, the proceedings are not open to public view and scrutiny.[279] Instead, they are evaluated and examined by the qualified personnel of the tribunals of the Church's universal judiciary.

Tribunal investigations that are concerned with the imposition of penalties are governed by laws of secrecy.[280] This type of trial may impose a punishment on a person for the violation of a law.[281] For instance, a priest may be brought to trial if accused of sexually molesting a child. If found guilty, the priest can be expelled from the clergy. If innocent, the charge is abandoned. Given the risk of harming a person's reputation, the obligation to observe secrecy in penal trials is paramount.

A marriage case is considered "contentious" in law, rather than penal. A matter is being disputed; a penalty is not being imposed. A case concerning marriage nullity affects a person's public status in the Church, that is, whether one is validly married or single. This is a matter of record; it is not a secret. So from the perspective of common sense, marriage cases are governed by strict confidentiality, not secrecy.[282] The distinction is important because it affects a person's reputation. Suppose a Catholic woman is an elected public official to the United States Congress and thus well known. It is also known that the congresswoman is divorced and civilly remarried outside the Church. Since the Church considers her married to one man while she is civilly married to another, she cannot approach holy communion. Yet suppose further that, after a time, the congresswoman's marriage is declared null, and she then marries her civil-law husband in the Church. The fact that she is married in the Church is a matter of Church record; it is not a secret. Therefore, if the congresswoman receives holy communion and a public response of scandal arises, a simple acknowledgment of this fact by Church authority would dispel the confusion.

The proceedings surrounding an investigation for a declaration of nullity are governed by strict confidentiality. Though the legal fact that a declaration has been granted in the affirmative is a matter of record in the Church, the facts of the case are not. The ground(s), the testimonies of the petitioner, respondent, witnesses and experts, and the proceedings themselves are not open to the general membership of the Church. This confidential component of the tribunal investigation is intended to protect the good names and reputations of all the parties involved.[283]

Marriage cases are often concerned with delicate matters. Such matters can cause public scandal and ruin someone's reputation if they become public. Court officials are obliged by their office and oaths to observe the laws of confidentiality and secrecy. For instance, judges are to maintain permanent secrecy concerning their discussions of a case.[284] Again, this is to prevent any harm or damage from being brought to bear on a person's reputation from the disclosure of such discussions. The Church requires high standards of professional behavior from its court officials. If any court official breaks the requirements of secrecy or strict confidentiality, he or she may be punished by the imposition of a penalty.[285]

Furthermore, if a judge is concerned that someone involved in the case who is not a court official may possibly

PART VII:

Personal and Family Effects of a Declaration of Nullity

Q. 76. What is a "putative" marriage?

Remembering that the ministers of marriage are the bride and the groom, the law declares that a **valid** marriage is brought about through: (1) the consent of the bride and groom, (2) legitimately manifested, (3) by those qualified according to the law (again, the bride and the groom).[288] When a wedding takes place, it is presumed that a marriage has come into existence.

However, if the consent of either the bride or groom was defective, then marriage was NOT brought about. If their consent was not legitimately manifested, then marriage was NOT brought about. If either the bride or the groom was unqualified by law to place consent, then marriage was NOT brought about. An ecclesiastical declaration of nullity decrees that, for a particular reason, a marriage had NOT come into existence on the wedding day, as everyone had presumed. A declaration of nullity declares a presumed marriage **invalid** in law.

A marriage that has been declared null by the Church is often called a **putative** marriage in law. The marriage is believed to have been valid by one or both of the parties, that is, one or both had celebrated the wedding ceremony in good faith. It is putative from wedding ceremony until the declaration, at which point it ceases to be putative.[289] What is the purpose of this legal term, *putative*? It is pastoral in nature. The principal effect of a putative marriage is that children born of or conceived during it are legitimate according to church law.

Q. 77. Is the grace of God operative in a putative marriage?

After a declaration of nullity has been granted, individuals may question, with good insight, the operation of God's grace in their putative marriage. If the Church has declared that the sacred bond of marriage did not come about on the wedding day, then where was God in the union? Where was the grace of God during those years of common life that the law calls a putative marriage?

These questions touch on the issues of the bond of marriage, sacramental vis-à-vis nonsacramental marriages and the nature of divine grace. First, the bond of marriage is not some separate reality existing above or alongside the partners. A wedding ceremony does not bring about a magical entity that exists beyond the parties. Rather, the bond of faithfulness expressed between husband and wife has a religious dimension. They enter into a covenant with God through the union of their love, whether it is a good and natural marriage or a Christian marriage. Thus an unbreakable "bond of unity" is established between the parties and God. God's grace is present in both good and natural marriages and Christian marriages.

As God himself is the author of marriage, he blesses the good and natural marriage. In the Old Testament this form of marriage modeled the covenant of love between God and his people, Israel. When a man and a woman have truly consented in love to live God's intended institution of marriage, he is present to them through grace. Good and natural marriages are ordered toward the good of the spouses and the procreation and education of children. The three goods of marriage—children, fidelity and a sacred lifelong commitment—are basic to the union. The essential properties of a good and natural marriage are unity and indissolubility, though this latter property is not as firmly established in a good and natural marriage as it is in a Christian marriage.

God's presence in a Christian marriage moves beyond that of a good and natural marriage. In this instance two baptized individuals marry in the Lord. When a baptized man and woman marry in Christ, their love is purified and fulfilled by God. A Christian marriage is not simply a sign and symbol of divine love. Rather, it is an effective sign, a fulfilled symbol and a real presence of the love of God as revealed in Jesus Christ.

When a Christian bride and groom marry, they invite God into their covenantal union of love. The sacramentality of marriage rests on this covenant of love between two people; a union that both reflects and shares in divine love. A married love makes present to the world Christ's union of love with his Church; it is in this graced, sacramental union that a family comes into being.

Sacraments are effective signs. This means they bring about, effect, confer what they signify. By the power of the Holy Spirit the real presence of God comes into the world. If a presumed sacramental marriage is declared to be null, then theologically God's presence was not conferred to the world through the union. The union was never established. In addition, if a good and natural marriage is declared null, the marriage was not symbolic of the faithful covenant of love between God and his people, Israel.

Theologically, a declaration of nullity states that the "bond of unity" between the parties and God was not established on the wedding day, as had been presumed. One or both of the parties did not establish a marriage, be that a good and natural marriage or a Christian marriage.

Does this mean that God was absent from the parties as they lived their common life, or that his gift of children was less than perfect? No. God's actual grace was present to each individual. His grace was not effective in their union, for the union had never been established. Rather, God's impelling love was at work in the individual lives of the parties; God never abandoned them in their common life. His grace sustained them as they experienced their lives together. In addition, as every child is a gift of divine love, parents were graced to cooperate in the creative power of God through procreation.

Was God's grace present to persons in a putative marriage? Without question—Yes.

Q. 78. Are the needs of children taken into consideration when a declaration of nullity is granted?

Yes.

Divorce may ultimately deprive children of their childhood: those years of dependence, education and sustenance. The stark reality of divorce is that it often hurts children. Though it may benefit the adults involved, contemporary research in various fields demonstrates that divorce is harmful to many children.

Divorce may cause children to lose a parent, and, so too, the love and nurturing that a marriage relationship should embody. It often forces children into poverty, and the side effects of poverty hold children captive. Their worlds are turned upside down as they face the harsh realities of a more difficult standard of life. A small but nonetheless growing number of children are homeless. Many endure poor quality and even dangerous child care. Some suffer from the consequences of poor health due to inadequate or no medical coverage. A great many fail to make it through the educational system.

Furthermore, the children of divorce perform more poorly academically and exhibit higher rates of behavioral and psychological problems than their counterparts in two-parent families. Aggression, social withdrawal, depression, lowered self-esteem, noncompliance with adult authority and fear of future relationships are problems characteristic of children who have experienced the marked parental discord of family disruption. These are the consequences of divorce. Children do not simply "bounce back" from its effects.

The Church cares deeply for children who experience the pain of their parents' divorce. Thus, there are two laws that address the needs of these children. First, when parents choose to marry in the Church, the law requires that the officiating priest or deacon must attain the permission of the bishop.[290] This permission is given when it is certain parents are fulfilling their natural obligations toward their children from any prior union.[291] Second, at the time of a declaration of nullity, the judge is to admonish parents regarding their moral and civil obligations for the support and upbringing of their children.[292] This judicial law is unambiguous: parents are expected to fulfill their parental responsibilities. Both laws are new to the 1983 Code, and both address the Church's concern for the welfare of children.

Can Church law demand that a parent love a child? Yes! The foundational law of the Church is love: love of God and neighbor. This command is at the heart of the parent/child relationship. The Church would be in disservice to children of divorce if it did not unequivocally demand, at the time of a declaration of nullity, that they receive parental love.

Q. 79. Does the tribunal process judge the character of the parties to a case?

No and Yes.

No, in the sense that the ministry of the tribunal is an impartial search for truth regarding the validity of a marriage. The legal presumption after a wedding ceremony is that a valid marriage has come into existence. Any petition that seeks to establish the contrary involves an impartial judgment concerning the facts as they have been presented. The ultimate judgment concerns the validity of the marriage, not the character of the parties.

Yes, in the sense that marriage involves the intentions and actions of the parties. The marital relationship is a lived experience between a man and a woman. Their intentions and actions as they lived their marriage are evaluated by court officials insofar as the facts of the case give evidence.

If a case is decided on defective consent due to partial simulation, a person's actions may be judged as morally offensive. For example, if it is revealed that a person excluded fidelity and had multiple affairs before and after the wedding, then he or she acted in a morally offensive manner. The person is correctly judged as having been adulterous. The person who excluded the good of a spouse and was emotionally, physically or sexually abusive has behaved in a repugnant manner. That person's behavior is judged reprehensible. The person who entered marriage through deceit was indeed dishonest. There are obvious moral judgments that have to be made by court personnel about the parties in light of their demonstrated behaviors during the marriage.

It is certainly uncomfortable for individuals to hear that their behavior is going to be judged "by the Church." However, it is important to remember that the ultimate judgment is whether the marriage in question is invalid. In no way does a declaration of nullity declare the moral state of the parties. It is not inquisitorial; that is, it is not a historical repeat of the Spanish Inquisition! The parties are not publicly branded "this or that" due to their intentions and actions. In fact, every case is confidential and, so, is never open to public scrutiny. Only the final decision regarding invalidity is public, as it effects a person's status in the Church (married or single).

Many tribunals have literature stating that the tribunal is not seeking to place blame on anyone or make judgments about anyone. This literature highlights that the ultimate judgment concerns the validity of the marriage. This pastoral approach to the process is not intended to be double-talk, for, as stated above, judgments about a person's intentions and actions are made. Rather, it is intended to calm anyone's fears by indicating that the tribunal investigation is neither public nor inquisitorial. However, a tribunal's pastoral approach to the process should not be interpreted as a moral waiver, if you will. The intentions and actions of individuals will be evaluated and judged. These judgments will be morally impartial, but not morally neutral.

In a tangible sense these judgments may impact on a person's right to marry again.

Q. 80. What is a "prohibition" regarding any future marriage?

The right to marry is a part of the natural law. However, it is not a limitless right; it may be restricted. Competent authorities may forbid a particular marriage or impose certain conditions on individuals before a marriage is celebrated.[293] This is called a **prohibition** (*vetitum,* in Latin). Different English words are employed by tribunals in the United States to express the Latin concept of *vetitum* to the parties. These are: prohibition, restriction, condition, counseling requirements and ban. In each case the person's fundamental right to marry is restricted.[294]

The prohibition declares a person may not marry in the Church for a particular reason. It is placed by authorities who minister in the administrative or judicial arenas of the Church. The judicial prohibition is imposed by an ecclesiastical judge or college of judges at the end of a matrimonial nullity trial. It will be lifted once certain conditions have been met by the party upon whom it has been placed. If a person marries under a prohibition, the marriage would be illicit (illegal according to law), though nonetheless valid.

Serious maladaptive behaviors or troublesome circumstances during the marriage may surface in the tribunal investigation. Thus, for the good of the individual, future spouse, possible children and the sanctity of the sacrament, these issues should be addressed by the parties before the Church permits any future marriage. For instance, suppose it was clear that the man was physically abusive to his wife and children during the time they lived together. The marriage was declared null on the ground of his defective consent—partial simulation against the good of the spouses. With the declaration both persons are free to marry again, unless either is restricted from doing so. In this case, the man would be prohibited from any future marriage in the Church until such time as those in authority believe that his abusive behavior is under control. He would have to undergo psychological therapy and evaluations. When the judge is satisfied from the experts' reports that the man's behavior is under control, he will lift the prohibition.

The placement of a judicial prohibition is left to the discretion of the judge(s). He or she evaluates the intentions and actions of the parties during the time that they lived together. As indicated in the example above, if issues of emotional, physical or sexual abuse were present, these actions would warrant a prohibition.

In addition, beliefs that are in opposition to the Church's teachings on marriage may also warrant a prohibition. For instance, if a woman's consent was defective due to an intention against fidelity, and her adulterous behavior was substantiated during the tribunal investigation, the judge may prohibit her from a future marriage. The condition for the removal of the prohibition would be that she intend any future marriage to be monogamous. If she refused to change her mindset, the prohibition would not be lifted.

Again, prohibitions exist to protect the good of the individual, future spouse and possible children, as well as the sanctity of marriage. It is the Church's attempt to balance the private and public dimensions of marriage—the individual's natural-law right to marry and the broader reality of marriage that supports the total welfare of the family and community at large.

Q. 81. What if it can be proven that the final decision was based on perjured testimony?

Individuals normally petition the Church for a declaration of nullity for one of two reasons: peace of conscience and/or the freedom to marry. At the root of the petition is the fact that the person questions the validity of his or her first marriage. He or she may believe in their heart that their marriage could not have been valid in light of all they experienced subsequent to the wedding ceremony. Often, a person seeks the Church's judgment to ease their conscience regarding the civil divorce from their spouse. In addition, the person may wish to marry again.

It is important to note that the Church affords divorced individuals the legal right to petition for a declaration of nullity. The institutional Church does not force individuals to enter into the tribunal process; rather, such individuals come forward of their own volition and submit a petition. If a person truly believes that their marriage is indeed valid, then he or she should not bring forth a petition that suggests otherwise. To do so would be cavalier at best, hypocritical at worst.

The spouses to a marriage can challenge its validity.[295] The burden of proof rests on the petitioner, not the Church. Once a petition has been initiated, the tribunal will begin its impartial search for truth. This search is based on the presumption that petitions are brought forward in honesty and good faith. Parties and witnesses swear an oath before God to tell the truth, the whole truth and nothing but the truth. This solemn oath is not to be taken lightly; in fact, the law imposes various penalties as punishment upon persons who commit perjury.[296]

The law states that cases concerning the status of persons (hence marriage) are never completely closed to future scrutiny.[297] Since the court decision rests upon the truthfulness of the parties and witnesses, the reality of sin cannot be overlooked. One cannot deny the possibility that a case is based on lies. Even the law admits this possibility. If it can be proven that a case was riddled with substantive lies and misleading information, the case can be reopened.[298] An affirmative decision based on perjured testimony will be overturned.

Q. 82. How is the process emotionally healing?

The ministry of the tribunal is pastoral when it is faithful to its nature as a ministry of justice and truth. Its ultimate task is the impartial search for truth. This path toward truth intersects the lives and the relationship of the persons who lived the marriage in question. When some parties move through the tribunal process, there is an opportunity for them to experience emotional healing. Admittedly, this is not the primary task of the tribunal, but it is a positive consequence in the search for truth.

The tribunal investigation is an emotionally difficult experience for petitioners hoping for an affirmative decision. Individuals need to present to the court their life stories. This can reopen old wounds resulting from a person's childhood and failed marriage that have not fully healed. In order to move on with their lives after a divorce, many individuals place an imaginary cap over their woundedness. The tribunal process hopefully removes this cap, and in doing so heals the wound.

Some tribunals request that petitioners write a personal history statement concerning the marriage before they present oral testimony. This writing process allows individuals to bring what is locked and hidden inside of themselves out into the open. Very often, this becomes a cathartic experience that allows them to view a painful situation in a new light, without the crippling effects of the past. They can begin to put healthy closure on the relationship and learn from past mistakes.

Oral testimony to the court regarding the marriage is another opportunity to experience healthy closure. When parties meet with their advocates, or the judge(s), they have an opportunity to address issues they may have repressed or feared. In addition, a review of the facts of the case and the sentence often affords a person objective feedback from others regarding the marriage. When a case is decided in the affirmative, it is hopefully healing for a person to hear the Church say: "You are not bound to this marriage, for these reasons."

Many individuals have suffered a great deal through the adverse circumstances of a troubled marriage. It is emotionally healing for them to know that the Church has looked objectively at their lived experience and decided in favor of nullity. This often verifies externally what they considered to be true in their hearts.

A case can also be emotionally healing for a respondent, aggrieved by the initial petition, when the case is decided in the negative. In this instance an individual feels vindicated when the Church upholds the validity of the marriage. The person believes in his or her conscience that the marriage is valid, and the decision upholds this belief.

The facts of the case may prove that a person simply changed his or her mind about the marriage well after the wedding ceremony. There is the example of the man who left his wife after twenty-five years of marriage, civilly divorced her and then married his young secretary. That man has the right to petition the court for a declaration of nullity; the burden of proof regarding invalidity rests on him. If the testimony of the opposed respondent and the witnesses does not support his claim of nullity, the decision will be in the negative, as the nullity of the marriage had not been proven by the petitioner. Even though the marriage was terminated civilly, a respondent in this situation feels emotionally supported in the Church's objective decision. The impartial search for truth confirms what she knows to be true in her heart.

Q. 83. How is the process emotionally harmful?

Again, the ultimate task of the tribunal is the impartial search for truth. This path toward truth intersects the lives and the relationship of the persons who lived the marriage in question. When some parties move through the tribunal process, there is an opportunity for them to experience emotional healing. Conversely, others experience pain and alienation. It is not the purpose of the tribunal to inflict pain and suffering, but this can be an unintentional consequence. The search for truth is not based on people's feelings regarding the eventual outcome, but rather the facts, circumstances and dynamics of the couple's marriage.

At times, a negative decision will be rendered by the court. This will be painful for a petitioner (and perhaps for the cooperating respondent) to hear. It means that the marriage in question remains valid in law. In the search for truth, the proof necessary to overturn the presumption of validity has not been demonstrated. Though there has been a civil divorce, the Church still considers the parties bound to the lifelong commitment they made on the wedding day. There are no consequences in the Church to the civil divorce. Though the parties are no longer living together, they are not free to marry again. This truth is obviously painful to bear.

At other times an affirmative decision will be very

painful to bear for an opposed respondent. It is not difficult to grasp the depth of pain for a person who has stayed in a terrible marriage for a long duration, only to have the Church declare it invalid. Yet, the search for truth can lead to that decision as well. Perhaps a couple was married for fifteen years with three children. Suppose that during the entire marriage the husband was adulterous and physically abusive to his wife and children. He cared only for himself and his next "alcoholic high." Yet, his wife stayed in the marriage because of her sacred commitment and for the sake of the children. Even though she knew he was "no good," it was her marriage, and she was not going to go back on her vows.

For this woman the civil divorce process that she endured would most likely be much less devastating than the Church's declaration of nullity. Such a decision might enrage her, and understandably so. This man, who had nothing to do with the Church and broke all of his vows, has the gall to petition the Church for a declaration of nullity so that he can marry again! By law the tribunal accepts his petition. In its search for truth an affirmative decision is reached because of the man's partial simulation, his intention against the good of the spouses. Marriage is not brought about through the consent of only one person. As much as her consent was healthy and active on the wedding day, his was not. Even though a prohibition is placed on him regarding any future marriage, her pain is not reduced. In cases such as these, there is no emotional healing, but rather pain and suffering for the respondent. Again, the truth is often painful to bear.

Few final judgments are agreeable to all the parties involved in a case, so emotional distress is often an inevitable aspect of tribunal ministry. Aside from the final judgment there are other factors in the process that may cause emotional distress to individuals—elements that are avoidable if addressed, but emotionally damaging to people when left unaddressed. In particular, there are three: (1) an insensitivity to individuals, particularly women; (2) a lack of awareness of the values underlying different cultures; and (3) an overreliance upon a process that is often geared to those articulate in English (in the United States) and prone to a legal jargon known only to a few.

First, some women may experience alienation from the outset of the tribunal process because most of the Church's judicial governance is rooted in the actions and decisions of men. This statement is not meant to be a critique of the system, for the Church operates out of its historical foundation and evolution. Nor is it meant to give credence to erroneous and misleading complaints that the Church's judiciary consist only of clerics. Such is not the case, as laymen and laywomen minister in tribunals.

Many women serve as judges, advocates and defenders of the bond of marriage. Women are directors of tribunals and serve in varying capacities on both professional and support staffs. The Church's integration of women into its judicial life is both laudable and commendable. This notwithstanding however, the personnel of the Church's judiciary consists primarily of men. So there is an inherent need on the part of these men to be especially sensitive to the concerns of women.

As with most legal systems, the Church's laws speak in a "juridical male voice." In other words, the ecclesial legal structure employs a language that often pertains to facts, rights, procedural actions and exceptions. This form of language can be perceived as cold and unfeeling. An overdependence on legal juridical terminology lacks a basic sensitivity to lived marital experience of many women and men. Tribunal personnel need to be sensitive to this deficiency in juridic language. If the tribunal process is perceived as concerned only with the facts of the case and the procedural application of law to these facts, parties can be harmed emotionally. Relationships are never devoid of emotions, sentiments and opinions. The expression of and the respect for these relational dynamics should not be minimized or overlooked by tribunal personnel. Likewise, if women and men are addressed and recognized solely through legal classifications, that is, their case names and protocol numbers, they will understandably conclude that the tribunal regards their marital experience as having little value. A lack of sensitivity to a person's feelings, especially those of pain, loss and suffering, will be construed as callous and unsympathetic.

Second, individuals will experience emotional pain if the tribunal process does not appreciate the particular culture within which the parties were raised and from which they chose marriage. There are obvious cultural differences among peoples from different countries. North Americans hold different worldviews of life and marriage than South Americans do, as Africans differ in these from Asians. There are also cultural differences among peoples who live within the same territorial boundaries. For example, people from New England have a different approach to life than people from Texas. Care must be taken to ensure that the tribunal process does not ignore these differences, or that tribunal personnel only act out of their own cultural experience and bias. Otherwise, injustice and emotional distress may be the results.

Finally, the United States tribunal process is often geared to those articulate in English and prone to a legal jargon known only to a few. This is an inherent weakness in the process because it can engender suspicion and thus harm. Admittedly, no process is perfect and resources are often limited. The ideal judicial environment would accommodate every language and every person's abilities. Though this is not feasible, efforts can be made to accommodate these concerns when possible. This will lessen the fear and frustration of those individuals seeking justice in a system they experience as alien. Care should also be taken to avoid an overreliance on technical canonical language. This language is foreign to the parties it is meant to serve. Tribunal personnel should recognize that an extensive use of canonical "legalese" intimidates people. The law exists to serve individuals and the Church at large, not the other way around.

Q. 84. How is the process spiritually crippling; spiritually healing?

It is important to reemphasize that the ultimate task of the tribunal is the impartial search for truth regarding a question about the validity of a marriage. This path toward truth intersects the lives and the relationship of the persons who lived the marriage in question.

Unfortunately, the tribunal process will be of little spiritual benefit to those who have been emotionally harmed by the final decision. Again, as stated in the above answer, such emotional harm is not the intention of the investigation, but at times an unavoidable consequence. Petitioners who receive a negative decision and opposed respondents who receive an affirmative decision are often wounded spiritually by these decisions. They feel betrayed by the Church. The final decision is spiritually offensive because it stands in opposition to their beliefs regarding the validity or invalidity of their marriages.

Persons who have lived their spiritual lives through the Church can feel rejected by the Church when the final decision stands in opposition to their beliefs. Though their belief in God is not shaken, their faith in his Church is lessened. In fact, they may be so offended that they leave the Church and take their children with them. When this happens, the community of the faithful loses its sons and daughters, as well as subsequent generations of followers. This is spiritually damaging to the entire Church and, sadly, a negative consequence of the search for truth.

However, when others move through the tribunal process,

there is an opportunity for them to experience spiritual healing. Admittedly, this is not the primary task of the tribunal, but it is a positive consequence resulting from its search for truth. More often than not, the process is spiritually healing to those who have found it emotionally healing: petitioners who have received an affirmative decision and opposed respondents who have received a negative decision.

Few tribunals have literature that refers to a person's spiritual life as he or she journeys through a tribunal investigation. Letters and pamphlets are devoid of spiritual reflections. Rather, the correspondence is very formal and legal. This style is intended to bespeak the seriousness of the process and to clearly articulate the Church's procedural laws. This helps to prevent any misunderstandings regarding a person's rights and responsibilities during the investigation.

Nonetheless, the Church's body of laws is ultimately rooted in the Gospel message of Christ, a message that encompasses his life, death and resurrection. As individuals move through the tribunal investigation, they can be encouraged to find solace in the Lord's passion. Just as the crucifixion was painful, so too, acknowledging the failure of a marriage and the loss of its hopes and dreams may also be painful.

Men and women are often emotionally scarred after a divorce. It's sobering to note that after the resurrection the Lord appeared to his disciples with the scars of the crucifixion on his body; not the wounds, but the scars. When you stop to think of it, you would imagine that his resurrected body would have been absolutely perfect—blemish free. However, his body was not; the scars were present.

Reflecting on this reality of the resurrected body, the believer grasps that every life is going to have its wounds. These wounds take different forms—broken relationships, adverse childhood experiences, addictions, abuse, sickness or death. We can choose to do what we will with these wounds. We can let the woundedness of our lives constantly pull us down, or we can hand it over to God and ask for his healing. Our faith teaches us that God will heal our wounds, but often the scars will remain. These emotional scars are memories of where we have been and who we are.

Bodily scars did not hold back the resurrected Christ, and our own emotional scars do not have to hold us back. Individuals who have gone through a tribunal investigation can be encouraged to use the process to their advantage spiritually through such reflections. Whether it be by tribunal or parish personnel, people should be encouraged to take insights they have gained during a tribunal investigation and turn them over to the Lord. A decision rendered in truth should ultimately enhance the spiritual well-being of a person.

Q. 85. Is the tribunal process scandalous?

No.

In its common usage the word scandalous refers to that which is disgraceful, shameful or improper. Since the tribunal process is an impartial search for truth that is both just and impartial, it cannot be scandalous. Yet, it is a lightning rod for scandal.

A scandal is a public disgrace. It is the damaging of a reputation. Anyone involved in the tribunal process (tribunal personnel or the parties and participants to a case) or anyone outside of the system (Catholics or non-Catholics who have had no experience with the tribunal) is capable of inciting scandal in regard to tribunal ministry. In particular, scandal is occasioned by (1) ignorance, (2) violations of procedural laws and (3) mutual disrespect.

The first avenue that opens the way to scandal is ignorance. When individuals are ignorant of the process, yet present themselves as informed, scandal occurs. Ignorance accounts for many of the common misconceptions surrounding declarations of nullity. The scandal wrought by this ignorance has devastating effects on the community at large.

It is the responsibility of the Church's teachers to educate the faithful in regard to the nature of marriage and for the Church's legal experts to educate the faithful in regard to the Church's judicial proceedings and structures. Conversely, it is the responsibility of others to be educated. The Church's "annulment process" is a flashpoint for many, in large part because it is tainted by the blind acceptance of falsehoods or the promotion of fallacious errors. Both are unacceptable. When offered, education shatters ignorance and thus renders scandal avoidable.

A second possible concern is the improper implementation of procedural law within tribunals. It is of paramount importance that individuals' procedural rights are protected and that the required procedural actions in trials are facilitated. If there are procedural improprieties in the processing of a case, justice is not served. In fact the law will invalidate the process when a person is not afforded his or her procedural rights.[299]

If an individual believes that his or her rights have been violated, the available recourse in law should be taken. If a violation has occurred, it should be corrected immediately. If a violation has not occurred, this should be explained to the party who believes otherwise. Clarity in these matters dispels confusion and suspicion. It also helps to diminish any resulting scandal, which only undermines public credibility in the Church's legal process.

A third avenue that can lead to scandal is the disrespect among persons involved in the process. Tribunal officials are constantly on guard to respect the emotions that tribunal proceedings may generate among the parties. Anger, indignation and fear are often expressed by parties to a case. Respect for these feelings is paramount. Legitimate expressions of exasperation and confusion require patience. Conversely, however, the toleration of abusive behavior is different; that is unacceptable.

In addition, parties to a case should avoid words and

actions of disrespect toward those who issue the final judgment of a case. The tribunal's impartial search for truth will lead to both affirmative and negative decisions. Parties will inevitably be aggrieved by these final decisions. There is nothing improper with taking exception to the decisions and anger is understandable. However, when exceptions include calumny and false accusations against those who render decisions, scandal inevitably abounds.

It is important to remember that no final decision rests on the judgment of one person. The minimum number of judges to decide a case is four. Exceptions can certainly be taken against the ultimate decisions of these men and women, but it should be done with respect, not defamation.

Tribunal proceedings are contentious in nature. Nonetheless, everyone involved should avoid damaging the reputation of others, as the harm done by such scandal can be immense.

PART VIII:

Dispelling Misconceptions

There are many misconceptions surrounding declarations of nullity. You may have heard some of them: The process takes years to complete; it costs thousands of dollars; it only matters who you are, or who you know! Misconceptions need to be confronted. So, let me address some of the more prevalent ones in order to dispel them.

Q. 86. Are "annulments" simply "Catholic divorces"?

No.

A civil divorce is a dissolution of a civilly valid marriage contract. No human power can dissolve a valid, consummated sacramental marriage. This statement is rooted in the Church's scriptural, theological and canonical traditions. A declaration of nullity is not a dissolution of marriage. Rather, it is a judicial pronouncement that a valid marriage had not been brought about on the wedding day, as the community of the faithful had presumed. The law states that marriage is brought about through: (1) the consent of the bride and groom, (2) legitimately manifested, (3) by those qualified according to the law (again, the bride and the groom).[300]

If a tribunal investigation determines that: (1) the consent was defective, then marriage was NOT brought about; (2) the consent was NOT legitimately manifested, then marriage was NOT brought about; (3) one or both of the persons was unqualified according to law, then the marriage was NOT brought about.

In each situation there is a judicial determination that a

valid marriage did not come into existence on the wedding day, as everyone had presumed. There is no dissolution of a marriage bond. A declaration of nullity is not a "Church divorce."

Q. 87. Does an "annulment" wipe the marriage away?

No.

The word annulment is not used in the universal law of the Church. It is not utilized because it is inappropriate. The word annulment implies that you are taking "something" and wiping it away. This is not what is being done when a declaration of nullity is granted. The Church is really declaring, in hindsight, that on the day of the wedding specific factors, such as defective consent, problems regarding its legitimate manifestation or the ineligibility of the bride or groom, prevented the two individuals from bringing about a valid marriage—as had been presumed. The ceremony is not wiped away—all the guests saw it happen. The relationship of husband and wife is not wiped away—that remains the relationship between the man and woman while they lived together.[301] The children are not wiped away—they remain legitimate.[302]

Rather, once a wedding has taken place, the legal presumption is that a valid marriage has been brought about. This presumption of validity stands in law, until contrary facts prove otherwise. The declaration of nullity affirms the contrary to be true. The burden of proof rests with the person who has initiated the petition before the tribunal. The tribunal can only declare whether or not it has been proven that the marriage was invalid from the start. The tribunal has no power to make the marriage null or void.

Q. 88. May a divorced Catholic who has not remarried receive holy communion?

Yes.

A belief to the contrary is usually rooted in one of two misconceptions: first, that a divorced person is excommunicated and so cannot receive holy communion; or second, that divorce negatively affects one's status in the Church and so, without a declaration of nullity, one cannot receive holy communion. Both misconceptions are false.

Unfortunately, many Catholics think that if they have divorced, even though they have not remarried outside of the Church, they are excommunicated and thus excluded from the reception of holy communion. This misunderstanding is derived from a Church council held in 1884 that imposed a penalty of excommunication on any Catholic in the United States who divorced and then remarried (note: this penalty has ceased to exist in Church law). The distinction between being divorced, and divorced and remarried outside the Church was lost in most people's minds. Divorce became synonymous with excommunication despite the fact that no one incurred this penalty for a divorce.

The law is clear: the divorced Catholic is not excommunicated and is free to receive holy communion.[303]

In addition, some individuals think they need a declaration of nullity after a divorce in order to receive holy communion. This is not the case either. Divorce only impacts upon one's status in civil law; it has no impact upon one's status in Church law. The State dissolves the civil contract of marriage with divorce, thus rendering the parties' civil-law status as single. However, the Church holds that a marriage is a valid union until proven otherwise in a Church court. A divorced couple remain married to each other in the Church, though they are obviously living apart after their civil divorce. Their status in Church law remains that of married persons.

Since the divorce does not impact upon one's status in the Church law, a divorced person is free to approach the eucharist. In fact, anyone who is divorced should be encouraged to find strength through the reception of holy communion. Such a person has probably lived through some traumatic experiences and, most likely, a painful separation from his or her spouse.

So as long as a divorced person has not remarried outside of the Church and he or she is not conscious of any mortal sin, that person can and should go to holy communion.

Q. 89. Is marriage the only sacrament that can be declared null?

No.

Declaring a sacrament null pertains not only to marriage, but to the other sacraments as well. Furthermore, just as the word *annulment* is inappropriate in regard to marriage, so too would it be inappropriate in regard to other sacraments. As legal procedures exist for a marriage case, so too do they exist for declaring the nullity of sacred ordination.[304] These cases are handled by the appropriate congregation in the Roman Curia or by a tribunal designated by it. Many of the laws governing a tribunal investigation of marriage would also apply to this process.[305] When a declaration of nullity is granted in regard to sacred ordination, the Church is stating in hindsight that certain factors prevented the bringing about of a valid sacrament of ordination—as had been presumed.

Let's turn to another sacrament for a clearer analogy to marriage—the eucharist. Unlike marriage, the minister of the eucharist is "solely a validly ordained priest."[306] On a particular Sunday you go to Church, but the pastor is away. A visiting priest enters in procession to the altar to lead the community in worship. The community prays together, the music is wonderful, the homily is terrific and everyone goes to holy communion. At the conclusion of the mass, you leave having had a prayerful experience.

Two weeks later it is discovered that the visiting priest wasn't a priest at all. It was a man named John Smith who played priest for the weekend! John could be severely punished in Church law for his deception, even including excommunication.[307] Suppose the deception became public and thereby scandalous. In this case a public declaration of nullity might be warranted.

Using hindsight, the Church would publicly declare the eucharistic consecration null and void. As the *Catechism of the Catholic Church* states: "Only validly ordained priests can preside at the Eucharist and consecrate the bread and the wine so that they become the Body and Blood of the Lord."[308]

The legal presumption that day at mass had been that bread and wine became the body and blood of Christ. Yet, in reality, that day bread and wine remained bread and wine. When everyone walked up to communion, all they received was a piece of bread and a sip of wine. There had been no sacramental effect at the celebration that day. The eucharistic consecration would be declared null. However, it would not be called an annulment of the eucharist.

Keeping the two sacraments (marriage and eucharist) in mind better situates and expresses why the word annulment is inappropriate. At that particular mass, people gathered together to pray. They were inspired by the music. They may have been moved by the man's talk. They certainly received grace from God. God heard their prayers. They received grace when they approached God with open hearts. All the declaration states is that there was no sacramental effect in regard to the eucharistic elements at that particular celebration. Why? Because the "minister" was not ordained.

The ministers of a sacramental marriage are the bride and groom, not the priest. In much the same way, a declaration of nullity in regard to marriage does not deny that one or both of the parties entered the marriage with good intentions. Presumably, they loved one another. They had hopes and dreams. They lived under the operation of God's grace. There were good times and bad times. If there were children born of their union, they are legitimate in law.

The declaration does not affect any of that. It simply states that the bond of marriage was not brought about that day. A valid sacramental marriage had not been brought about, as had been presumed. There may have been a defect of consent on the part of one or both ministers; the consent was not legitimately manifested; or, one or both of the parties may have been incapable, according to law, of exchanging consent. The legal presumption of a valid marriage in each instance yields to a declaration of nullity.

Q. 90. Is it true that marriages of long standing, with children, can be declared null?

Yes.

The Church affords any divorced person the right to petition for a declaration of nullity. The length of the marriage or presence of children does not prevent the acceptance of a petition.

However, with that said, the longer the duration of marriage, the more difficult it is to overturn the presumption. Every case requires witness testimony. The presumption of validity cannot normally be overturned on the testimony of one party.[309] There must be corroborative proof.[310]

So, common sense indicates that the further one moves away from the wedding day, the more difficult it is to overturn the presumption of validity. Witnesses have died or are unable to be located, or they may no longer remember the circumstances because consent was exchanged so long ago. Hence, it is more difficult for a petitioner to prove nullity if the marriage had been long-standing in duration.

Nonetheless, as the Church affords individuals the right to petition, individuals may exercise this right.

Q. 91. Does the Church declare null the marriages of non-Catholics (whether Christian or unbaptized)?

Yes.

If both the bride and groom are baptized non-Catholics, the marriage is a Christian marriage, that is, sacramental. If only one party or neither party is a baptized non-Catholic, the marriage is a good and natural marriage, or nonsacramental. In either case the marriage is recognized as valid in Church law.

Non-Catholics are not bound by the Church laws that govern the form of marriage for Catholics. Obviously, the Church would not require two baptized Presbyterians to approach a Catholic priest to witness their exchange of vows. As long as these two Presbyterians exchange consent, their marriage is considered a valid sacrament by the Catholic Church.

Once the Catholic Church recognizes a marriage as a valid sacrament, any question of invalidity must come before a Church tribunal if a Catholic is involved in a future marriage. So, if two baptized Presbyterians marry and subsequently divorce, and the divorced man now wishes to marry a Catholic woman, he is not free to do so. He would only become free if the Church were to issue a declaration of nullity for his first marriage.

Furthermore, if two Jews marry before the rabbi, that is considered a good and natural marriage. It is viewed as valid, though nonsacramental, in Church law. Any question of invalidity or dissolution must come before a Church tribunal.

These types of petitions normally occur when a divorced Protestant or nonbaptized person wishes to marry a Catholic. The community of the faithful is concerned for its individual members, as the marriage of any member of the Church affects all the members. The number of formal cases involving non-Catholics that are brought before tribunals will depend upon the religious demographics of the area.

Q. 92. Is every case brought before a tribunal granted in the affirmative?

No.

It is important for divorced individuals to know that the Church affords them the legal right to petition for a declaration of nullity.[311] No one has a right to a declaration of nullity; rather, the right exists to petition for one.

The burden of proof is on the petitioner. The legal presumption is that the marriage in question is valid.[312] Certainly, if a marriage has ended in divorce, something has gone wrong. The tribunal investigation seeks to determine whether anything was defective at the start. The answer may be in the affirmative. It also may be in the negative.

Q. 93. Is a marriage rendered null by the Church after the decision of only one court?

No.

The Church declares a marriage null only after two concordant affirmative decisions. It is incorrect to state that a marriage has been declared null after the decision of only one court. Due process involves the decision of the First Instance Court (usually known as the diocesan tribunal) and the decision of an appellate level court (either provincial or Roman). A case is pending under procedural law until the Appellate Court's decision brings about a final judgment.[313]

In addition, the minimum number of judges to decide a case is four. These numbers vary depending on the circumstances of the case and the process of appeal.

Q. 94. Do declarations of nullity take years to complete?

No and Yes.

Tribunal officials begin with the premise that the marriage in question is indeed valid. Anything contrary is going to have to be proven. The burden of proof is on the petitioner. There are certain time limits throughout the proceedings in which individuals have the right to take actions or respond.[314] Cases are tried in the order they are presented.[315] On average, a marriage proceeding is to take approximately one and a half years, in accord with the law.[316] However, this time frame varies among tribunals throughout the world. Practical considerations such as personnel resources and procedural circumstances such as the delay in witness testimonies are responsible for these variations.

Q. 95. Don't declarations of nullity cost thousands of dollars; doesn't the Church make money from them?

No—to both issues.

There are court costs associated with the processing of trial proceedings.[317] The cost is not a donation to the Church. Rather, it is a fee for services rendered. The moneys support the operating expenses of the Church court, such as salaries, office supplies and building expenses. In most dioceses there are various fees for differing types of cases. In some dioceses there are no fees associated with tribunal processes.

Formal petitions involving investigations of a defect of consent comprise the most common types of cases. The assessment of fees in these cases normally reflects only a part of the actual expenditures. Some United States dioceses do not assess the parties any fees. In these places the diocese fully subsidizes its tribunal. In other dioceses the parties are assessed fees that cover a percentage of the actual case costs, and the diocese assumes the rest. No diocese supplies the tribunal's annual operating expenses solely through the assessment of fees.[318] Such hard data undercut the fallacious notion that the Church makes money from declarations of nullity. In fact the opposite is true.

At times, parties cannot assume the cost of even the nominal fees. This does not affect the processing of the case. There is discretion on the judge's part regarding a reduction of the fee.[319] In cases of serious financial need, the fee may be waived. If there is a need to pay in installments over time, the person is accommodated.

Q. 96. Is it easy to receive a declaration of nullity?

No.

The process is involved. The petitioner is asked to submit detailed testimony. The tribunal contacts the former spouse. Witnesses are required. An expert in the field of psychology may be required for an assessment. It is not an easy process. However, it is not impossible either.

The misconception that it is thought to be easy to receive a declaration of nullity may rest in the increased number of such declarations over the past twenty years, especially in the United States. In 1968 the tribunal in Boston, Massachusetts processed ten cases involving defective consent. In 1996 the same tribunal processed over seven hundred of these cases. The increase is due to substantial changes in the procedural law of the Church; for example, cases may be handled by a single judge rather than a tribunal panel of three judges.

The process is thorough and just, and respects the procedural rights of all parties involved.

Q. 97. Do declarations of nullity render children illegitimate?

No.

When a marriage of parents is declared null by the Church, many people are confused about its impact upon the legitimacy of the children. In fact, a judicial sentence that declares the nullity of a marriage does not affect the legitimacy of children born of that union. Any statement or belief to the contrary is simply wrong.

Tragically, it is a common misconception that a declaration of nullity renders children illegitimate in the eyes of the faith community. The laws of the Catholic Church clearly state that this is not the case.[320] The misconception is derived from two perspectives:

First, this harmful fallacy is derived from the use of the word *annulment*. Again, the word is inappropriate when discussing proceedings of nullity before a Church tribunal. In fact, the word *annulment* is not used in the law of the Church. Rather, a trial proceeding that declares the nullity of marriage is more aptly referred to by the phrase, "declaration of nullity."[321]

As stated earlier, the word *annulment* implies that you are taking "something" and wiping it away. When this erroneous word is applied to a declaration of nullity, it signifies that the entire relationship between the spouses is wiped away or erased, including the legitimacy of children. This connotation underscores the inappropriateness of the word; nothing is "erased." In Church law a marriage that is declared null is thereafter referred to as a "putative," or "supposed," marriage.[322] It was a marriage contracted in violation of an impediment, or with a condition or defective consent, but entered in good faith on the part of one or both of the contracting parties.

Second, the misappropriation of the term *illegitimate* indicates a misunderstanding of legitimacy. *Legitimacy* is a term used by many legal systems throughout the world. The term indicates knowledge of a child's paternity. The maternity of a child (the Latin word for *mother* is *mater*) is usually obvious. The issue of the child's paternity (the Latin word for *father* is *pater*) can be less so. The term *legitimacy* connotes that a child's father is the husband of the child's mother at the time of conception or birth. In no way could a declaration of nullity deny a child's paternity. At the time of birth, the legally presumed relationship between the child's father and mother was indeed that of husband and wife. A declaration of nullity does not deny this, so the legitimacy of the child cannot be affected.

Legitimacy is one of the first issues addressed to parties who are involved in tribunal procedures regarding marriage. The misconception is so pervasive that it needs to be corrected. Unfortunately, it is not uncommon for spouses who have obtained a civil divorce to continue ex-spousal hostilities in the postdivorce situation. These hostilities can surface in the parental relationship, and clearly the children suffer. There are few things more heartwrenching to tribunal officials than to discover that a child has been told by a parent that the Church is going to render him or her "illegitimate" through the granting of a declaration of nullity. Informed parents who make such a statement have allowed anger at another adult to triumph over the well-being of the child.

The church promotes the dignity of children in many arenas, including its legal structures. It is imperative to state clearly and unambiguously that children born of a marriage that has been declared null remain legitimate. There is no room for misconceptions.

Q. 98. How does the Church manifest its care for children after a divorce and before a remarriage?

The Church is very concerned for the welfare of the children of divorce. The Church insists that parents do all in their power to provide for the physical, social, cultural, moral and religious upbringing of their children.[323]

Judges admonish parents to fulfill both their civil and ecclesial obligations to children when a declaration of nullity is granted.[324] Parents must also verify that their obligations to children are met before they remarry in the Church.[325] Parish personnel preparing parents for remarriage address the fulfillment of parental responsibilities.

Q. 99. When it comes to an affirmative decision, is it true that it only matters who you are or who you know?

No.

The name or position of the petitioner, respondent or any witness does not matter. Everyone is treated with the same procedural rights in law. No one is penalized for being well known. No one is penalized for being unknown. Everyone is treated fairly and in accord with the norm of law. In fact, no officer of the court is permitted to take part in a case in which there is a family relationship, close friendship, animosity or the desire to profit or avoid a loss.[326] This law exists to protect the integrity of the process and to avoid any suggestion of collusion.

Q. 100. Does the Church care about what a person has endured in the marriage?

Yes.

The Church cares a great deal for persons who have suffered in marriage. Petitioners, respondents and witnesses are treated with pastoral care and sensitivity by tribunal personnel.

In addition, when a declaration is granted, both parties are free to marry again in the Church UNLESS either is restricted from doing so.[327] The right to marry is based in the natural law. However, it is not a limitless right—certain restrictions may be placed upon its exercise. They are called "conditions," "restrictions" or "prohibitions" (in Latin, *vetita*).

A tribunal investigation may surface patterns of physical, sexual, chemical or emotional abuse. Patterns of self-destructive behavior may also be evident. Individuals may suffer from untreated, though diagnosed, psychological illnesses. These instances, and others, may warrant the imposition of a restriction regarding a future marriage until the issues are satisfactorily addressed. The good of the individual, future spouse and children, and the sanctity of the sacrament demand this cautionary tool.

Q. 101. There have been so many declarations of nullity granted in the United States recently; is justice really being served?

Yes.

Tribunals across the United States are operative so that individuals may vindicate their rights. The bishops of our country have invested significant personnel and resources to ensure compliance with the Church's jurisprudence and procedural law. Unfortunately, such an investment in justice is not as evident in other parts of the world. This is one reason why the numbers appear to be significantly higher in the United States. In addition, cultural factors in the United States and the revision of the Church's procedural laws also account for the rise in numbers.

There has been much written within the community of the faithful that first-world countries—especially the United States—have fallen into the trap of materialism and hedonism. The American culture is commonly referred to as pagan.

If this particular critique is accepted, then its cultural effects must also be acknowledged. One obvious consequence influences the potential spouses who live in this culture. They are formed and raised in this milieu. This is a culture that views nothing as permanent. This is a culture that promotes sexual excess. This is a culture that perpetuates a contraceptive mentality. Our children and youth are bombarded with these pagan cultural values.

The Church presumes that, at the time of marriage, the bride and groom are committing to permanence, fidelity and conjugal love. That is the presumption. However, one can readily see in this culture how the presumption could be overturned subsequent to a wedding ceremony.

In the last twenty years, the numbers of declarations of nullity are much higher in this country than they had been in the past. This is due to the fact that the procedural laws governing marriage cases in the Court of First Instance were changed in the late 1960s. The appellate system was also somewhat streamlined. Furthermore, Roman jurisprudence was expanded in the light of the teaching of the Second Vatican Council. Cases could be heard on new grounds.

The greater number of declarations of nullity are due to procedural law changes, an expansion of jurisprudence and cultural changes in our society. It is interesting to note, however, that fewer than 20 percent of those who can petition, do petition. The vast majority of divorced Catholics do not.

Since over 80 percent of divorced individuals in the United States remarry, one can only assume that most do so outside of the Church. It is this reality that undermines the community of the faithful, not the superficial notion that there are too many declarations of nullity.

With the continued commitment of bishops, canon lawyers and dedicated personnel who staff them, tribunals in the United States will continue to administer the Church's justice. The legal work of these individuals ultimately fulfills the supreme law of the Church: the salvation of souls.[328]

GLOSSARY

The following terms are used without elaboration in the preceding text; working definitions of them are proposed below:

1983 Code of Canon Law: A codified system of universal laws for the Latin Church; these 1,752 laws were promulgated by Pope John Paul II in 1983; the majority of these laws are referred to as human laws, that is, enacted on the Church's authority and therefore alterable; a few pertain to divine and natural law.

Divine law: Laws believed to be drawn directly from God's revelation and hence considered to be unalterable.

Illicit: Referring to an action not legally permitted or authorized; the action is unlawful, but nonetheless valid; hence an effect is brought about in law.

Invalid: Referring to an action without legal force; such an action is null.

Latin Church: Diverse liturgical traditions or rites, collectively referred to as Ritual Churches, exist within the

Catholic Church. These include the Latin, Byzantine, Alexandrian or Coptic, Armenian, Maronite and Chaldean Churches. The Latin Church is the largest of these Ritual Churches. It is primarily composed of the Roman rite. The majority of Catholics in the United States belong to this rite and so identify themselves as Roman Catholics. But the Latin Church is also comprised of the rites of certain local churches, such as the Ambrosian rite, as well as the rites of certain religious orders (see the *Catechism of the Catholic Church*, nos. 1200–1203).

Natural law: Laws that are considered to be drawn from God's creation, reason or religion; they are ethically binding in human society.

Valid: Referring to an action that is effective in law; it may or may not have been legally permitted (licit or illicit), but nonetheless it has produced the effects stipulated by the law.

NOTES

Introduction

1. *Catechism of the Catholic Church,* no. 1628 and 1983 Code of Canon Law, canon 1103.

2. Throughout each section of this book, endnote references are made to the pertinent canons on marriage and trial law from the 1983 Code of Canon Law, should the reader wish to investigate further.

Part I: The Right to Marry

3. *Catechism of the Catholic Church,* no. 1603.
4. Canon 1055.
5. Canon 1055.
6. Canon 1056.
7. Canon 1058.
8. Canons 1073–1082.
9. Canons 1083–1094.
10. Canon 1059; cf. also canon 11.
11. Canon 1057.
12. Canons 1063–1072.
13. Canon 1075.
14. Canon 1085.

15. Cf. canons 1142, 1143.1 and 1148–1150.

16. Canon 1084.

17. Canon 1091.

18. Canon 1092.

19. Canon 1093.

20. Canon 1094.

21. Canon 110.

22. Canon 1083.1.

23. Canon 1086.

24. Canon 1056.

25. *Catechism of the Catholic Church*, no. 1635.

26. Canon 1087.

27. Canon 277.1.

28. Canon 573.

29. Canon 1078.

30. Canon 1088.

31. Canon 1192.1.

32. Canon 607.

33. Canon 1078.

34. Canon 134.

35. Canon 1088.

36. Canon 1089.

37. Canon 1090.

38. Canon 1090.1.

39. Canon 1090.2.

40. Canon 1078.

41. *Catechism of the Catholic Church*, nos. 2384–2385.

42. Canon 1056.

43. *Catechism of the Catholic Church*, nos.1640 and 2382.

44. Canon 1141.

45. Andrew Cherlin, *Marriage, Divorce, Remarriage,* rev. ed. (Cambridge, Mass.: Harvard University Press, 1992) 24.

46. National Child Support Assurance Consortium, *Childhood's End: What Happens to Children When Child Support Obligations Are Not Enforced* (Toledo, Ohio: The Association for Children for Enforcement of Support, Inc., 1993) 6–7.

47. Barbara Dafoe Whitehead, "Dan Quayle Was Right," *The Atlantic Monthly,* April 1993, 58–60.

48. Barbara Dafoe Whitehead, *The Divorce Culture* (New York: Alfred A. Knopf, Inc., 1996) 95–96.

49. *Catechism of the Catholic Church,* no. 1606.

50. Canon 1136.

51. Canon 1674, 1°.

Part II: The Public Dimensions of Marriage

52. *Catechism of the Catholic Church,* no. 1603.

53. Canons 1055.1; 1056; 1095; 1099; 1101.2; 1134; 1135 and 1136.

54. *Catechism of the Catholic Church,* no. 1603.

55. Canon 1055.2.

56. *Catechism of the Catholic Church,* no. 1623.

57. Canon 1057.

58. Canon 1060.

59. Canon 1141.

60. Canon 1061.

61. Canon 1142.

62. Canons 1697–1706.

63. Canon 1055.

64. Canon 1056.

65. Canon 1141.

66. Canons 1143–1147.

Part III: The Diamond of Consent

67. Canon 1057.

68. *Catechism of the Catholic Church,* no. 1626.

69. Canons 1095–1107.

70. Canon 1096; cf. also canon 1099.

71. Canon 1097.

72. Canon 1098.

73. Canon 1095, 1°.

74. Canon 1095, 2°.

75. Canon 1095, 3°.

76. Canon 1101.

77. Canon 1102.

78. Canon 1103.
79. Canons 1674 and 1675.
80. Canon 1677.3.
81. Canons 1095–1103.
82. Canon 19.
83. Canons 1419, 1438–1439, 1442–1445.
84. Canon 1095, 1°.
85. Canon 1095, 2°.
86. Canon 1095, 3°.
87. Canon 1096.1.
88. Canon 1096.2.
89. Canon 1097.1.
90. Canon 1097.2.
91. Canon 1098.
92. Canon 1099.
93. Canon 1101.2.
94. Canon 1101.1.
95. Canon 1055.1.
96. Canon 1056.
97. Canon 1099; cf. canon 1055.2.
98. Canon 1101.1.
99. Canon 1101.2.
100. Canon 1055.1.
101. Canon 1101.1.
102. Canon 1101.2.
103. Canon 1056.
104. Canon 1101.1.
105. Canon 1101.2.
106. Canon 1056.
107. Canon 1101.1.
108. Canon 1101.2.
109. Canon 1055.1.
110. Canon 1101.1.
111. Canon 1101.2.
112. Canon 1055.
113. Canon 1101.1.
114. Canon 1102.1.
115. Canon 1102.2 and .3.
116. Canon 1101.1.

117. Canon 1103.
118. Canon 1057.
119. Canons 1156–1160.
120. Canons 1156–1158.
121. Canon 1159.

Part IV: The Church As Witness

122. Canon 1057.
123. Canon 1057, and canons 1108–1123; 1127.
124. Canon 1108.
125. Council of Trent, decree, *Tametsi* (1563).
126. Canon 144; cf. canon 1108.1.
127. *Catechism of the Catholic Church,* no. 1630.
128. Canon 1108.2.
129. Canon 1112.
130. Canon 1108.
131. Canon 1055.
132. *Catechism of the Catholic Church,* nos. 1213 and 1617.
133. Canon 1057.
134. Canon 1060.
135. Canon 1055.
136. Canon 1057.
137. Canon 1109.
138. Canons 1108–1123, 1127.
139. Canon 1060.
140. Cf. canon 1057.
141. Canons 1156–1165.
142. Canons 1156–1160.
143. Canons 1161–1165.
144. Canons 1156–1158.
145. Canon 1159.
146. Canon 1164.
147. Canons 1161.1 and 1163.
148. Canon 1057.1.
149. Canon 1162.1.
150. Canon 1161.3.
151. Canon 1161.1 and 2; 1164.

Part V: The Tribunal and Court Officials

152. Canon 1400.1.
153. *Catechism of the Catholic Church,* no. 1629.
154. Canon 221.1.
155. Canon 1674, 1°.
156. Canons of Book VII of the 1983 Code.
157. Canons 1419–1437.
158. Canons 1438–1441.
159. Canons 1442–1445.
160. Canon 1419.1.
161. Canons 1419 and 1420.
162. Canons 1405.1, 1° and 4°.
163. Canon 1673, 1°–4°.
164. Canon 1421.2; cf. also canon 228.1.
165. Canons 1420–1421.
166. Canon 1425.
167. Canon 1425.4.
168. Canon 1421.2.
169. Canon 1425.3.
170. Canon 1448.1.
171. Cf. canon 1456.
172. Canons 1450–1451.
173. Canon 1453.
174. Canons 1465–1466.
175. Canon 1598.1; cf. canon 1455.
176. Canon 1611.
177. Canon 1610.
178. Canon 1483.
179. Canon 1490.
180. Canon 1484.
181. Canon 1481.
182. Canon 1561.
183. Canon 1678.1, 2°.
184. Canon 1601.
185. Canons 1481 and 1482.
186. Canon 1490.
187. Canons 1484 and 1485.
188. Canon 1481.

189. Canon 1559.
190. Canon 1485.
191. Canon 1486.
192. Canon 1432.
193. Canon 1435.
194. Canons 1533 and 1561.
195. Canon 1678.
196. Canon 1628.
197. Canon 1601.
198. Canon 1602.
199. Canon 1574.
200. Canon 1680.
201. Canon 1577.
202. Canon 1575.
203. Canon 1581.1.
204. Canon 1575; cf. canon 1581.2.
205. Canon 1577.
206. Canon 1579.
207. Canon 1580; cf. canon 1649.1, 1°.

Part VI: Participating in the Tribunal Investigation

208. Canons 1501 and 1502.
209. Canons 1674, 1°, 1476 and 221.1.
210. Canon 221.2.
211. Canons 1501–1504.
212. Canon 1477.
213. Canon 1477.
214. Canon 1592.
215. Canon 1593.2.
216. Canon 1481.
217. Canon 1547.
218. Canons 1551 and 1552.
219. Canons 1554 and 1555.
220. Canon 1553.
221. Canon 1549.
222. Canon 1550.
223. Canon 1548.

224. Canon 1547.
225. Canon 1560.
226. Canon 1561.
227. Canons 1559, 1561 and 1678.2.
228. Canon 1562.
229. Canon 1453.
230. Canon 1453.
231. Canon 1501.
232. Canon 1502.
233. Canons 1502–1503.
234. Canon 1620, 4°.
235. Canon 1505.1.
236. Canon 1502.
237. Canons 1505 and 1506.
238. Canon 1507.1.
239. Canon 1512.
240. Canon 221.1.
241. Canon 1511.
242. Canon 1620, 4° and 7°.
243. Canon 1509.
244. Canon 1510.
245. Canon 1508.2.
246. Canon 1598.1.
247. Canon 1620, 7°.
248. Canon 220.
249. Canon 223.2.
250. Canon 1455.3.
251. Canon 1598.2.
252. Canon 1599.
253. Canon 1608.
254. Canon 1689.
255. Canon 1614.
256. Canon 1615.
257. Canon 1614.
258. Canon 1682.2.
259. Canon 1682.1.
260. Canon 1632.1.
261. Canon 1453.
262. Canon 1444.1, 1°.

263. Canon 1632.1.
264. Canon 1682.1.
265. Canon 1441.
266. Canon 1453.
267. Canon 1465.1.
268. Canon 1609.5.
269. Canon 1465.3.
270. Canon 1465.2.
271. Canons 201–203.
272. Canon 1467.
273. Canon 1649.
274. Canon 1649.1.
275. Canon 1649.1, 1°.
276. Canon 1649.1, 2°.
277. Canon 1649.1, 3°.
278. See *Proceedings of the Fifty-Eighth Annual Convention* (Washington, D.C.: Canon Law Society of America, 1996) 478–89.
279. Canon 220.
280. Canon 1455.
281. See canons of Book VI.
282. Cf. canon 1455.1.
283. Canon 220.
284. Canon 1455.2.
285. Canon 1457.
286. Canon 1455.3.
287. Canon 1368.

Part VII: Personal and Family Effects of a Declaration of Nullity

288. Canon 1057.
289. Canon 1061.3.
290. Canon 134.
291. Canon 1071.1, 3°.
292. Canon 1689.
293. Canons 1071, 1684 and 1685; cf. canon 223.2.
294. Canon 18.
295. Canons 1476 and 1674.
296. Canon 1368.

297. Canon 1643.
298. Canon 1644.
299. Canon 1620.

Part VIII: Dispelling Misconceptions

300. Canon 1057.
301. Canon 1061.3.
302. Canons 1137 and 1138.
303. Cf. canon 221.3.
304. Canons 1708–1712.
305. Canons 1400–1670.
306. Canon 900.
307. Canon 1378.
308. *Catechism of the Catholic Church,* no. 1411.
309. Canon 1573.
310. Canons 1678–1680.
311. Canons 1476 and 1674.
312. Canon 1060.
313. Canons 1682–1684.
314. Canons 1465–1467.
315. Canon 1458.
316. Canon 1453.
317. Canon 1649.
318. See *Proceedings of the Fifty-Eighth Annual Convention* (Washington, D.C.: Canon Law Society of America, 1996) 478–89.
319. Canon 1649.1.
320. Canons 1137 and 1138.
321. Canons 1673, 1677.3, 1682, 1684 and 1690.
322. Canon 1061.3.
323. Canon 1136.
324. Canon 1689.
325. Canon 1071.1.
326. Canon 1448.
327. Canons 1684 and 1685; cf. canon 223.2.
328. Canon 1752.

INDEX OF PROPER NAMES AND OF SUBJECTS TREATED IN THE QUESTIONS

The numbers listed below refer to Questions, not to pages. Boldface numbers refer to main references for entries.